A DICTIONARY OF
JAPANESE FINANCIAL TERMS

A DICTIONARY OF

JAPANESE FINANCIAL TERMS

DOMINIC WILLIAMS

JAPAN
LIBRARY

A DICTIONARY OF JAPANESE FINANCIAL TERMS

JAPAN LIBRARY
Knoll House, 35 The Crescent
Sandgate, Folkestone, Kent CT20 3EE

Japan Library is an imprint of Curzon Press Ltd
St John's Studios, Church Road, Richmond, Surrey TW9 2QA

First published 1995
© Dominic Williams

British Library Catalogue in Publication Data
A CIP catalogue entry for this book
is available from the British Library

ISBN 1–873410–11–5   Case
      1–873410–12–3   Paperback

Publisher's Note
We are grateful to the Scottish Centre for Japanese Studies,
University of Stirling, for their invaluable technical
assistance in the making of this dictionary.

Printed and bound in England by Redwood Books, Trowbridge, Wiltshire

Contents

Preface

This dictionary is the result of many years of working in the technical translation field involving Japanese; it is a project that essentially evolved out of a personal need to create a reference data base, especially relating to the financial markets, that would be readily accessible and provide the insights and nuances expressed in Japanese financial terminology that could be understood in the West. Hence the extensive use of context examples, many of which have historical cultural roots, which it is hoped will help make day-to-day work (both on and off screen) in interpreting Japanese financial and market activity more meaningful.

From this point of view, in dictionary terms, it is a hybrid and will continue to evolve, through future editions, to reflect both the changing terminology of the financial market place and also take into account what has been overlooked in this first edition. It goes without saying, therefore, that proposals for new entries will always be welcome.

The second section, offering English-romaji references, is a much more modest undertaking and will surely be expanded in future editions.

The last section, sets out key data indices relating to Japanese economic and industrial performance which are drawn from Japanese sources and therefore, in themselves, offer valuable benchmarks when making international comparisons, interpreting direction, or anticipating change.

PART ONE

JAPANESE - ENGLISH

A

ageru 上げる raise, produce
kō-shūeki o ageru 高収益を上げる make a quick profit

aitai baibai 相対売買 negotiated trading, cross-trade
also *aitai* 相対

ajitsuke 味付け support buying
also *ajitsuke-gai* 味付け買い / Support buying 'adds' 付け 'flavour' 味 or 'seasoning' to stimulate the market when a stock is bearish. 味付け is also a term found in cooking, where it means literally 'seasoning'

Ajia アジア Asia
Ajia darā sai アジア・ダラー債 Asian-dollar bond / *Ajia-gata* アジア型 Asian-type / *Nihon nado Ajia-gata kaihatsu moderu no seiko* 日本などアジア型開発モデルの成功 The success of an Asian-type model of development, such as Japan's

akaji 赤字 deficit
lit. 'red' 赤 'figures' 字 , 'in the red' / *Bei-bōeki akaji* 米貿易赤字 US trade deficit / *bōeki akaji kakudai* 貿易赤字拡大 rise in trade deficit (lit. 'expansion' 拡大 in trade deficit) / *aka-nishin mokuromi-sho* 赤ニシン目論見書 red herring prospectus (lit. 'red' 赤 'herring' ニシン 'prospectus' 目論見書)

akinai 商い trading
hibakari akinai 日計り商い daytime trading / *kaiten akinai* 回転商い overtrading / *kappatsu na akinai* 活発な商い brisk trading / *akinai-usu* 商い薄 thin trading / *Shinki zairyō-busoku de, akinai-usu no naka, shijō wa yōsumi-kibun ga tsuyoi.* 新規材料不足で、商い薄の中、市場は様子見気分が強い Players are keeping to the sidelines in thin trading due to a lack of incentives

akunuke 灰汁抜け with no more adverse factors
lit. with the 'harshness' 灰汁 'removed' 抜け / A situation in which there are no more immediate bad factors 灰汁 for a stock, and the stock price, which until the present has continued to fall, touches bottom and can only, from now on, climb. This term is found also in cookery, when the unpleasant odours or flavours 灰汁

of an ingredient are removed 抜け prior to cooking

aku-zairyō　悪材料 adverse factors, bearish factors, bad news

akuijishon　アクイジション acquisition
also *gappei* 合併

akyūmyrēshyon hōshiki　アキューミュレーション方式
accumulation system

amai　甘い sweet, dull, easy
amami zairyō 甘み材料 sweetener

Amekkusu　アメックス American Stock Exchange
The full Japanese term is *American Kabushiki Torihikisho* アメリカン株式
取引所 (also *Torihikijo* 取引所)

anarisuto　アナリスト analyst
kōnin shōken anarisuto 公認証券アナリスト a CFA (Chartered Financial
Analyst)

andāraitā　アンダーライター underwriter

antei　安定 stability
antei haitō 安定配当 stable dividends / *antei kabu* 安定株 investment
holdings (lit. 'stable' 安定 'stock' 株) / *antei kabunushi* 安定株主 a strong,
long-term stockholder / *antei sōsa* 安定操作 stabilizing transaction, stabilizing
operation / *antei-teki* 安定的 stable / *Antei-teki na saiyō o nentō ni oita* 安
定的な採用を念頭に置いた Put stable employment first

anzen　安全 safety
anzen shihon 安全資本 secure capital

aoru　煽る bull the market, add fuel to, fan (flames)
*Rōdōshō wa 24-ka, fukyō no aori de raishun sotsugyō yotei no joshi
gakusei ga, shū shoku de sabetsuteki na atsukai o ukeru osore ga aru
koto kara...* 労働省は24日、不況の煽りで来春卒業予定の女子学生が、就
職で差別的な扱いを受ける恐れがあることから…、 The Ministry of Labour
said on the 24th that as the recession bites, it is feared that girl students planning
to graduate next Spring may be treated in a discriminatory manner with respect to

finding a job... / *Zaiko seiri ga susumi, shinausu-kan ga shijō shinri o aorihajimeta* 在庫整理が進み、品薄感が市場心理を煽り始めた Inventories adjustment continued, and scarcities began to add fuel to the market's fears

ao-tenjō 青天井 topless, skyrocketing

aozora shijō 青空市場 open-air market
lit. 'blue' 青 'sky', *sora* 空 'market' 市場

apāto アパート apartment, flat

atama-uchi 頭打ち reaching a ceiling
lit. the 'head' 頭 'hits' 打ち the ceiling

-atari 当たり per
hitokabu-atari no rieki 一株当たりの利益 earnings per share

aya あや technicality
lit. 'complication' e.g. *iro-iro aya ga aru* 色々あやがある be very complicated; 'subtlety' e.g. *kotoba no aya:* 言葉のあや shade of meaning / *aya-modoshi* あや戻し technical rally, technical rebound / *ayaoshi* あや押し technical reaction

B

baibai 売買 buying and selling, trading, dealing
lit. 'sell' 売 and 'buy' 買 / *aru meigara o torihikisho de baibai suru koto no kyoka* ある銘柄を取引所で売買することの許可 the admission of a security to be traded on the stock exchange / *itaku baibai* 委託売買 brokerage, agency transaction / *jiyū kyōsō baibai shijō* 自由競争売買市場 free auction market / *kyōsō baibai* 競争売買 (also *seri baibai* 競り売買) auction / *baibai-daka* 売買高 turnover, trading volume / *baibai ichinin chūmon* 売買一任注文 discretionary order / *baibai seiritsu-bi* 売買成立日 date of transaction

baikai バイカイ crossing order

baishū 買収 acquisition, purchase, takeover
baishū kaisha (also *baishū gaisha*) 買収会社 a company which acquires another

baikyaku 売却 sale, disposal
kotei shisan baikyaku 固定資産売却 sale of capital assets

ban 板 board
keiji ban 掲示板 quotation board, New York Stock Exchange. The quotation board of the New York Stock Exchange, and by extension, a nickname for the Exchange itself

baransu-gata tōshi shintaku バランス型投資信託
balanced fund

baratsuki バラつき difference, disparity
Pafōmansu no men de wa kakusha-goto no baratsuki ga hageshikatta パフォーマンスの面では各社ごとのバラつきが激しかった There were wide disparities between the various companies in respect of performance

bareru バレル (oil) barrel

bātsu バーツ the baht
Tai-bātsu タイ・バーツ the Thai baht

Bei- 米 America, American
Bei-doru 米ドル US dollar / *Bei-bōeki* 米貿易 American trade / *Bei-kinri* 米金利 American interest rates

benchi māku ベンチ・マーク benchmark
also *kijunten* 基準点 and *sokutei kijun* 測定基準

bensai 弁済 payment, repayment, settlement
bensai o ukeru 弁済を受ける to receive payment

besshi no jōto shōsho 別紙の譲渡証書 detached assignment
lit. 'separate paper' 別紙, 'transfer' 譲渡 'certificate' 証書

betsudan yokin 別段預金 special deposit

12

bōeki 貿易 trade

Kanzei Bōeki Ippan Kyōtei 関税貿易一般協定 General Agreement on Tariffs and Trade (generally referred to as GATT, and in Japanese, Gatto ガット) / *jiyū bōeki* 自由貿易 free trade / *bōeki akaji* 貿易赤字 trade deficit (lit.'trade' 貿易 'red' 赤 'figures' 字) / *bōeki akaji kakudai* 貿易赤字拡大 rise in trade deficit (lit. 'expansion' 拡大 in trade deficit) / *bōeki kuroji* 貿易黒字 trade surplus (lit. 'trade' 貿易 'black' 黒 'figures' 字) / *bōeki kuroji kakudai* 貿易黒字拡大 rise in trade surplus (lit. 'expansion' 拡大 of trade surplus) / *bōeki tōkei* 貿易統計 trade statistics

bōraku 暴落 slump, heavy fall, collapse

kabuka bōraku 株価暴落 shares crash, heavy fall in share prices

boshū 募集 offering, placement, distribution

boshū annaisho 募集案内書 bond circular, offering circular (with regard to the US Securities Exchange Commission)

buai 歩合 rate, ratio

kōtei buai 公定歩合 official discount rate (ODR)

buchō 部長 divisional director

see also *shachō* 社長 president / *fuku-shachō* 副社長 vice-president / *kaichō* 会長 chairman / *senmu* 専務 (also *senmu torishimariyaku* 専務取締役) executive director / *jōmu* 常務 (also *jōmu torishimariyaku* 常務取締役) managing director / *kachō* 課長 sectional head

budomari 歩留り yield, yield rate

bukka 物価 prices (of commodities)

bukka jōshō 物価上昇 price rises, rises in the cost of living / *bukka kyōran* 物価狂乱 spiralling price rises, inflation out of control / *kouri bukka shisū* 小売り物価指数 retail price index / *shōhisha bukka shisū* 消費者物価指数 consumer price index

bukken 物件 property

riisu bukken リース物件 leased property / *riisu bukken chinshaku-ryō* リース物件賃借料 rent for leased property

bunjō 分讓 allotment

in the sense of buying or selling a flat *apāto* アパート in a purpose-built block, mansion マンション or condominium

bunkatsu-barai 分割払い instalment

bunsan 分散 spread, diversification
kawase risuku o bunsan suru 為替リスクを分散する spread the risk arising from exchange rate fluctuations / *bunsan tōshi* 分散投資 diversified investment

bunseki 分析 analysis
shōken bunseki 証券分析 security analysis

buzumi 歩積み compensating deposit
see *ryōdate* 両建て

C

*chakuchi 着値 misreading for *chakune*

chakune 着値 c.i.f. price

chein sutoā チェイン・ストアー chain store

chihō 地方 local, municipal, prefectural
chihō jichitai sai 地方自治体債 local government bond / *chihō jichitai saimu shōken* 地方自治体債務証券 (see *chihō sai* 地方債) / *chihō sai* 地方債 (from *chihō jichitai saimu shōken* 地方自治体債務証券) municipal or local government bonds, prefectural bonds

*chikin 地金 misreading for *jigane*

chinpu-ka 陳腐化 obsolescence

chinshaku 賃借 hiring, leasing
chinshaku-ryō 賃借料 rent / *riisu bukken chinshaku-ryō* リース物件賃借料 rent for leased properties

chō 兆 trillion (i.e. thousand billion, million million)

182-chō 7,903-oku en 182兆7903億円 Yen 182.7903 trillion, Yen 182,790.3 billion

chō 庁 government agency
Chūshō Kigyō Chō 中小企業庁 Small and Medium Enterprises Agency / *Keizai Kikaku Chō* 経済企画庁 Economic Planning Agency (EPA)

chōbo-jō rieki 帳簿上利益 paper profit, book profit

chochiku 貯蓄 saving, savings
chochiku ginkō 貯蓄銀行 savings bank

chōki 長期 long term
chōki fusai 長期負債 fixed liabilities, fund debt / *chōki ritsuki kokusai* 長期利付き国債 long-term government bonds / *chōki shihon torihiki shijō* 長期資本取引市場 capital market (c.f. *tanki kin'yū shijō* 短期金融市場 money market)

chō-kikan 長期間 long term
chō-kikan ni watatte 長期間に渡って over the long term / *Kabuka ga heikin kabuka o chō-kikan ni watatte ryōga suru* 株価が長期間に渡って平均株価を凌駕する The share price, over the long term, exceeds the average price

chokin 貯金 savings
yūbin chokin 郵便貯金 post office savings

chōki-teki 長期的 long-term

chōsei 調整 adjustment
Kinri Chōsei Shingikai 金利調整審議会 Interest Adjustment Council / *kōzō chōsei* 構造調整 structural adjustment / *Kyoninka ya kisei nado, doko made seifu ga kan'yo suru no ka no rūru o hakkiri sase, takoku-kan de chōsei shite takoku no shisutemu o chōwa sasete iku* 許認可や規制など、どこまで政府が関与するのかのルールをはっきりさせ、多国間で調整して多国のシステムを調和させて行く To clarify the rules as to how far Government will take part in certification and regulation, and to harmonize various countries' systems through international cooperation / *zaiko chōsei* 在庫調整 inventory adjustment (lit. 'stock' 在庫 'adjustment' 調整)

chōtanki 長短期 long- and short-term
chōtanki no saikensha 長短期の債権者 long- and short-term creditors /
chōtanki no saikensha yori kashitsukerareta shihon 長短期の債権者より
貸し付られた資本 Capital financed by long- and short-term creditors

chōtatsu 調達 raising (funds), procurement (of commodity)
kin'yū chōtatsu 金融調達 financing, raising funds / *shikin chōtatsu* 資金調
達 raising capital

chōwa 調和 harmony
chōwa suru 調和する harmonize / *Kyoninka ya kisei nado, doko made
seifu ga kan'yo suru no ka no rūru o hakkiri sase, takoku-kan de chōsei
shite takoku no shisutemu o chōwa sasete iku* 許認可や規則など、どこ
まで政府が関与するのかのルールをはっきりさせ、多国間で調整して多
国のシステムを調和させて行く To clarify the rules as to how far Government
will take part in certification and regulation, and to harmonize various countries'
systems through international cooperation

chōzei-ryoku 徴税力 taxing power
lit. 'imposing taxes' 徴税 'power' 力

chū 注 N.B
This is found at the bottom of a table of statistics, and will often appear as *chū 1*
注1 even where there is only one note

chūkai 仲介 intermediary
chūkai-ka 仲介化 intermediation

chūki 中期 medium-term
chūki ritsuki kokusai 中期利付き国債 medium-term coupon government
bond (lit. 'medium term' 中期 'with interest' 利付き 'government bond' 国債) /
chūkoku 中国 (also *chūki kokusai* 中期国債) medium-term government bond
funds

chūmon 注文 order
chūmon o sabaku 注文を捌く handle an order / *kaitsuke chūmon* 買い付け
注文 buying order / *mu-kigen chūmon* 無期限注文 open order / *nariyuki
chūmon* 成り行き注文 carte blanche order, order without limit, market order
(lit. 'order' 注文 which is left to the 'course of events' 成り行き) / *sashine
chūmon* 指し値注文 limited (stop) order, straddled order / *torikeshi chūmon*

取り消し注文 cancel order / *uri chūmon* 売り注文 offer / *uritsuke chūmon*
売り付け注文 selling order / *chūmon no shikkō* 注文の執行 the execution of
an order

chūshō kigyō 中小企業 small and medium enterprises

lit. 'medium' 中 and 'small' 小 'enterprises' 企業 / *Chūshō Kigyō Chō* 中小
企業庁 Small and Medium Enterprises Agency

D

dai 台 numerical classifier for machines etc.

heikin gekkan hanbai daisū 平均月間販売台数 average number of
machines sold per month / *-dai ni noseru* 台に乗せる reach the mark /
1,000-en-dai ni noseru 1000 円台に乗せる reach the Yen 1,000 mark /
daikin 代金 cost, price, money for / *tochi daikin* 土地代金 money for land /
tochi daikin jōto teitō 土地代金譲渡抵当 mortgage money / *dairinin* 代理
人 agent, representative / *zaimu dairinin* 財務代理人 fiscal agent

-daka 高 *taka* 高, which see

uriage-daka 売上高 sales

dareru だれる to be dull, inactive

Kai ichijun-go, dareru (TSE) 買一巡後、だれる TSE: Dull, after brief buying

dashi-te 出し手 lender

*Kōru mujōken-mono rēto wa zenshumatsu-hi kawarazu no 4% (dashite)
ni sueokareta* コール無条件ものレートは前週末比変わらずの４％（出し
手）に据え置かれた The rate for unconditional call loans was 4% selling,
unchanged from the previous weekend, and therefore deferred

debaisu デバイス electronic component

debaisu gyōkai デバイス業界 component industry

dedokoro 出所 source, authority

also *shussho* 出所 or *shutten* 出典 / Usually found at the bottom of a table or
chart crediting the source of the statistics

dekidaka 出来高 sales volume

demawaru 出回る arrive on the market, be moving

denki 電気 electricity, electric power (as a category of equities)
  denki-gasu 電気ガス electrical power and gas (as a category of equities)

denki 電器 electrical machinery, electrical tools, electricals
  (as a category of equities)

deru 出る take action on the market, enter the field as a player
  doru-uri ni deru ドル売りに出る engage in dollar-selling

diirā ディーラー dealer
  diirā kaisha (also *diirā gaisha*) ディーラー会社 dealer firm

Doku- 独 Germany
  Doku-maruku 独マルク German Mark

donka 鈍化 edging down, slowing down

doru ドル dollar
  Bei-doru 米ドル US dollar / *Go-doru* 豪ドル Australian dollar / *Honkon-doru* ホンコン・ドル Hong Kong dollar / *Kanada-doru* カナダ・ドル Canadian dollar / *Shingapōru-doru* シンガポール・ドル Singaporean dollar / *Taiwan-doru* 台湾ドル Taiwanese dollar / *doru-daka* ドル高 a high dollar, the dollar's appreciation / *doru-date saiken* ドル建て債券 American dollar bonds / *doru heikin hō* ドル平均法 dollar cost averaging (see also *kappu tōshi* 割賦投資 investment instalment) / *doru-yasu* ドル安 a cheaper dollar, the falling dollar

E

Ei- 英 UK
  Ei-pondo 英ポンド sterling / *Eikoku Sangyō Renmei* 英国産業連盟 Confederation of British Industry (CBI)

eigyō 営業 operations, running a business

eigyō-hi 営業費 operating costs / *eigyō hōkokusho* 営業報告書 business report / *eigyō-jitsu* 営業日 business days / *eigyō rieki* 営業利益 operating profits / *eigyō shūeki* 営業収益 operating volume

en 円 yen

tsumitate en 積立円 reserved yen / *endaka* 円高 the high yen, the yen's appreciation / *endate* 円建て in yen terms, converted into yen / *endate gaisai* 円建て外債 'samurai' bond, yen-denominated bond issued in Japan by non-Japanese issuers / *en'yasu* 円安 a cheaper yen, a falling yen

enzetsu 演説 speech

kichō enzetsu 基調演説 keynote speech

F

fuandamentaru anarisuto ファンダメンタル・アナリスト fundamental analyst

fudō 浮動 floating

fudō gyoku 浮動玉 (also *fudō kabu* 浮動株) floating supply / *fudō kabu* 浮動株 (also *fudō gyoku* 浮動玉) floating stock

fudōsan 不動産 real estate, immovables

lit. 'non-' 不 'move' 動 'assets' 産 / *fudōsan tampo-tsuki saiken* 不動産担保付き債券 debenture (lit. 'real estate' 不動産 'secured' 担保付き 'bond' 債券)

fuederaru fanzu フェデラル・ファンズ federal funds

fukin 付近 narrow range, region

Tōkyō owarine fukin de yoritsuita 東京終値付近で寄付いた The dollar opened at almost the same level as Tokyo's close

fuku-shachō 副社長 vice president

see also *shachō* 社長 president / *kaichō* 会長 chairman / *senmu* 専務; also *senmu torishimariyaku* 専務取締役 executive director

fukyō 不況 recession, (business) depression, slump, slack business
fukyō-kan ga hirogaru 不況感が広がる business conditions give way to recession

fumikiru 踏み切る to launch
Beikoku ga kōtei buai no hikisage ni fumikitta haikei ni tsuite 米国が公定歩合の引下げに踏み切った背景について Behind the lowering of the discount rate by the US

funki 奮起 be braced, be roused to action, be inspired to
Debaisu gyōkai ga kōshūeki o agete iru naka, shirikon mēkā no funki to danketsu ga hitsuyō to narō デバイス業界が高収益を上げている中、シリコン・メーカーの奮起と団結が必要となろう At a time when the component industry is making quick profits, silicon manufacturers will need to brace themselves and stick together

funō 不能 inability
shiharai funō 支払い不能 insolvency (lit. 'inability' 不能 'to pay' 支払い)

furikō 不履行 non-fulfilment, non-observance, breach
saimu furikō 債務不履行 failure to meet obligations

furan フラン franc
Futsu-furan 仏フラン French franc / *Suisu furan* スイス・フラン Swiss franc

furō フロー flow
kabuka kyasshu-furō ritsu 株価キャッシュ・フロー率 price cash-flow ratio / *kyasshu furō* キャッシュ・フロー cash-flow / *kyasshu furō ritsu* キャッシュ・フロー率 cash-flow ratio

fusai 負債 debt, indebtedness, liabilities
ryū dō fusai 流動負債 current liabilities

fushin 不振 stagnation

fu-tekiō-ka 不適応化 inadequacy

Futsu- 仏 France
Futsu-furan 仏フラン French franc

futsū 普通 ordinary
> *futsū kabu* 普通株 ordinary stock (UK), common stock (US) / *futsū shasai* 普通社債 straight bond / *futsū waribiki* 普通割引 ordinary discount / *futsū yokin* 普通預金 ordinary deposit

G

gaika 外貨 foreign currency
> *gaika kakutoku* 外貨獲得 earning foreign currency / *gaika yokin* 外貨預金 foreign currency deposits / *gaikoku kawase shijō* 外国為替市場 foreign exchange (forex) market / *gaikoku sai* 外国債 foreign bond, external bond / *gaisai* 外債 foreign bonds (short for *gaikoku saiken* 外国債券) / *gaishi* 外資 foreign capital

gaku 額 amount, value
> e.g. value of imports as opposed to volume *ryō* / *gakumen* 額面 face value, nominal par value / *gakumen ijō de torihiki suru* 額面以上で取引する sell at a premium / *gakumen ika de torihiki suru* 額面以下で取引する sell at a discount / *meimoku gakumen kabushiki* 名目額面株式 nominal par value stock

*ganbon 元本 misreading for *ganpon*

ganpon 元本 principal
> *ganpon hensai hōshiki* 元本返済方式 principal repayment method

gappei 合併 acquisition
> also *akuijishion* アクイジション / *kyūshū gappei* 吸収合併 take-over

gein ゲイン gain
> *kyapitaru gein* キャピタルゲイン capital gain

gen 元 yuan
> *Chugoku-gen* 中国元 the Chinese yuan

genbutsu 現物 spot, cash and similar items
> *Kai ichijun-go wa saitei kaishū ni tomonau genbutsu kabu-uri ni*

osareta 買い一巡後は裁定解消に伴う現物株売りにおされた After brief buying, market players were forced to sell spot shares while cancelling arbitrage / *genbutsu sai* 現物債 cash bonds / *genbutsu torihiki* 現物取引 trading for cash

gen'eki 減益 reduced profits

genka 減価 discount
genka muyō 減価無用 do-not-reduce (DNR) order / *genka shōkyaku* 減価償却 depreciation / *genka shōkyaku hikiate kin* 減価償却引当金 depreciation reserve, allowance for depreciation, accrued depreciation

gen-kabushiki 原株式 underlying share

genkai seisan kosuto 限界生産コスト marginal cost of production

genkin 現金 cash
genkin-ka 現金化 cash realization / *genkin kanjō* 現金勘定 cash account / *genkin shisan kachi* 現金資産価値 cash assets value / *genkin zandaka* 現金残高 cash holdings, cash balance

genmō 減耗 wasting
genmō shisan 減耗資産 wasting assets

*genpon 元本 misreading for *ganpon*

gensai 減債 sinking
gensai shikin 減債資金 sinking fund / *gensai shikin saiken* 減債資金債券 sinking funds bond

gensaki 現先 bond repurchase agreement
gensaki shijō 現先市場 bond repurchase market

gensan 減産 reduced production
Zurekomu keiki kaifuku de gensan, zaikochōsei kyōka e ずれ込む景気回復で減産、在庫調整強化へ reduced production and further inventory adjustment as recovery recedes

gensen 源泉 source
gensen kazei 源泉課税 pay-as-you-earn, tax assessment at source

genshō 減少 fall, drop, decline

gen-tegata 原手形 underlying bills

gen'yu 原油 crude (oil)
Nanoka no Rondon gen'yu supotto shijō no Hokkai Burento soba wa kougoki 七日のロンドン原油スポット市場の北海ブレント相場は小動き North Sea Brent crude oil prices rose slightly on the London spot market on the 7th August

genzai 現在 present
genzai kakaku 現在価格 present value

geraku 下落 fall, drop, decline, lose ground

gijutsu 技術 technology

giketsu-ken 議決権 voting power
at a shareholders' general meeting / *giketsu-ken kabunushi* 議決権株主 voting shareholder / *giketsu-ken shintaku* 議決権信託 voting trust

gimu 義務 duties (of a company, trustee, boardmember)
kenri gimu 権利義務 rights and duties

ginkō 銀行 bank
chochiku ginkō 貯蓄銀行 savings bank / *sōgo ginkō* 相互銀行 mutual savings bank / *sōgo ginkō* 総合銀行 'do-all' bank / *toshi ginkō* 都市銀行 city bank / *yokin ginkō* 預金銀行 deposit bank / *ginkō hikiuke tegata* 銀行引受手形 banker's acceptances

Gō- 豪 Australia
gō-doru 豪ドル Australian dollar

goba 後場 afternoon session
Goba ni hairu to, kawase ga 1doru=127en zenpan de kougoki to nari... 後場に入ると、1ドル=127円前半で小動きとなり... In the second half, the exchange rate moved slightly to the lower reaches of $1=¥127

gōben 合弁 merger, consolidation

also *kigyō gōben* 企業合弁 merger, consolidation / *kyūshū gōben* 吸収合弁 merger (through absorption) / *shinsetsu gōben* 新設合弁 merger (though creation) / *gōben kaisha* (also *gōben gaisha*) 合弁会社 joint company

gomu ゴム rubber

gomu yōgyō ゴム窯業 rubber & ceramics (as a category of equities)

gūhatsu 偶発 contingency

gūhatsu saimu 偶発債務 contingent liabilities, secondary liabilities / *gūhatsu sonshitsu tsumitate-kin* 偶発損失積立金 contingency reserve

gyaku 逆 opposite, counter

gyaku-gawase 逆為替 reverse remittance / *gyaku-sashine* 逆指値 counterbid / *gyaku-sashine chūmon* 逆指値注文 stop-order, stop-loss order

gyōkai 業界 an industrial circle

debaisu gyōkai デバイス業界 component industry circles / *kin'yū gyōkai* 金融業界 financial circles

gyoku 玉 shares bought or sold

gyoku-atsume 玉集め (also *kabu-atsume* 株集め) accumulation / *gyoku torihiki* 玉取引 trading in shares / *tairyō gyoku torihiki* 大量玉取引 block transaction

gyōseki 業績 business results

renketsu gyōseki 連結業績 consolidated results / *tandoku gyōseki* 単独業績 parent company results

gyōsha 業者 broker

hikiuke gyōsha 引受業者 underwriting broker, issuing house / *hikiuke gyōsha kanji* 引受業者幹事 syndicate manager / *shōken gyōsha* 証券業者 broker / *gyōsha-kan no torihiki* 業者間の取引 inside market, wholesale market / *gyōsha-kan torihiki kakaku* 業者間取引価格 inside price, wholesale price

H

hadaka nedan 裸値段 net price
lit. 'naked' 裸 'price' 値段

haigo 背後 background, behind
Beikoku wa Nihon shijō ni sannyū dekinai haigo ni, Nihon no keizai shakai shisutemu sono mono ga aru koto ni kizuita 米国は日本市場に参入出来ない背後に、日本の経済社会システムそのものがある事に気づいた The US noticed that behind the fact that it cannot be a player in the Japanese market lies Japan's very economic and social system

haitō 配当 dividend
mi-shiharai haitō 未支払い配当 arrearage / *yūsen haitō* 優先配当 stipulated dividend, preferred dividend / *haitō ochi* 配当落ち dividend cuts, ex-dividend / *haitō ritsu* 配当率 dividend rate / *haitō seikō* 配当性向 pay-out ratio / *haitō shishutsu* 配当支出 dividend requirements / *haitō-tsuki* 配当付き with dividend, dividend-on

hakabu 端株 odd-lot shares, broken lot
hakabu torihiki 端株取引 odd-lot trading

hakkō 発行 issue, launch, float
seifu hakkō yūka shōken 政府発行有価証券 gilt-edged security / *shibo hakkō* 私募発行 private placement / *shinki hakkō* 新規発行 new offering / *hakkō-bi* 発行日 effective day (lit. 'day' 日 of 'issue' 発行) / *hakkō kaisha* (also *hakkō gaisha*) 発行会社 issuing company / *hakkō kikan* 発行期間 offering period / *hakkō-sha* 発行者 issuer / *saiken hakkō-sha* 債券発行者 bond issuer / *hakkō shijō* 発行市場 primary market (lit. 'issuing' 発行 'market' 市場, as opposed to secondary market *ryūtsū shijō* 流通市場, lit. 'circulating' 流通 'market' 市場) / *hakkō shōken* 発行証券 issue / *hakkō shōken o yudaneru* 発行証券を委ねる award an issue (e.g. to an underwriting group)

hanbai 販売 sales
madoguchi hanbai 窓口販売 'over-the-counter' sales / *hanbai dan* 販売団 selling group / *hanbai tesūryō* 販売手数料 selling concessions, selling commission

hanekaeri kinyū 跳ね返り金融 'boomerang' yen financing

han'i 範囲 range, scope
tekisei kabuka han'i 適正株価範囲 intrinsic range

hanpatsu 反発 rebound

hanraku 反落 reactionary fall, setback
kyū-hanraku 急反落 a sharp setback, a strong reaction

hantō 反騰 a reactionary rise

happyō 発表 announcement, publication

haraikomi 払い込み paid-up, paid-in
haraikomi shikin 払い込み資金 paid-up capital, capital stock paid in

haraimodoshi 払い戻し repay
yokin no haraimodoshi 預金の払い戻し the repayment of deposits

hasan 破産 bankruptcy, business failure

*hashikabu 端株 misreading for *hakabu*

hatten 発展 development
hatten tojōkoku 発展途上国 developing country(ies)

hatsubai 発売 putting on the market, launch a product

heikin 平均 average
kabuka heikin 株価平均 average share price / *kajū heikin* 荷重平均 weighted average / *Nikkei Heikin* 日経平均 Nikkei Stock Average / *heikin sen* 平均線 average

hendō 変動 change
saishō hendō bun 最小変動分 minimum fractional change

hensai 返済 repayment

-hi 費 expense, cost, charge

kaihatsu-hi 開発費 development expense / *kotei-hi* 固定費 fixed cost, fixed charge

-hi 比 compared with
zengetsu-hi 前月比 month-on-month / *Kashidashi-kin wa zengetsu-hi 625-oku-en-zō no 219-chō 9,928-oku-en datta* 貸出金は前月比625億円増の219兆9928億円だった The value of loans totalled 219,992.8 billion yen, up 62.5 billion yen month-on-month / *zennendo-hi* 前年度比 compared with the previous fiscal year / *zenshūmatsu-hi* 前週末比 compared with the previous weekend

hibaishū gaisha 被買収会社 see *hibaishū kaisha*

hibaishū kaisha 被買収会社 a company bought, acquired
also *hibaishū gaisha* (lit. A 買収会社 is a company which acquires another. 被 corresponds to the English '-ee' as in 'lessee', 'divorcee'; the original concept of 被 is 'passive' or 'suffer')

hibakari akinai 日計り商い daytime trading

hibu 日歩 interest rate
(the daily formula) of *sen* 銭 per ¥100, per dime rate, interest per dime / *urikata hibu* 売方日歩 seller's per dime rate

hi-chūkai-ka 非仲介化 disintermediation

hi-hakkō kabushiki 非発行株式 outstanding stock

hi-jōjō 非上場 unlisted
hi-jōjō shōken 非上場証券 unlisted securities

hiekomu 冷え込む to cool
Shigatsu mo kojin shōhi ga hiekomi... 四月も個人消費が冷え込み... In April also personal consumption cooled...

hika 比価 parity
kingin hika 金銀比価 parity of gold and silver

hikeru 引ける to close
koyasuku hiketa 小安く引けた finished weak / *hikene* 引け値 closing price

hikiage 引上げ raising
kōtei buai no hikiage 公定歩合の引上げ raising of official discount rate (ODR)

hikiate kin 引当て金 reserve
genka shōkyaku hikiate kin 減価償却引当て金 depreciation reserve

hikisage 引下げ reduction
kanzei hikisage 関税引下げ tariff reduction / *kōtei buai no hikisage* 公定歩合の引下げ lowering of the official discount rate (ODR) / *Beikoku ga kōtei buai no hikisage ni fumikitta haikei ni tsuite* 米国が公定歩合の引き下げに踏み切った背景について Behind the lowering of the discount rate by the US

hikishime 引締め tightening, restraint, squeeze, restriction
kin'yū no hikishime 金融の引締め financial restraint, credit squeeze

hikiuke 引受け underwriting, purchase, subscription, guaranty
Kōsha Sai Hikiuke Kyōkai 公社債引受協会 Bond Underwriters Association / *hikiuke gurūpu* 引受けグループ an underwriting group / *hikiuke gyōsha* 引受け業者 underwriting broker, issuing house / *hikiuke gyōsha kanji* 引受け業者幹事 syndicate manager / *hikiuke kanji* 引受け幹事 managing underwriter / *hikiuke kanji tesūryō* 引受け幹事手数料 managing fees / *hikiuke-ken* 引受け権 subscription right / *kabushiki hikiuke-ken* 株式引受け権 subscription right / *shinkabu hikiuke-ken-tsuki saiken* 新株引受け権付き債券 bond with subscription right, bond with pre-emptive right / *shinkabu hikiuke-ken-tsuki shasai* 新株引受け権付き社債 warrant bond / *shinkabu yūsen hikiuke-ken* 新株優先引受け権 privileged subscription right / *hikiuke-kin* 引受け金 underwriting, subscription / *hikiuke-nin* 引受け人 underwriter / *hikiuke shidan* 引受け師団 underwriting division, underwriting syndicate / *hikiuke tegata* 引受け手形 acceptance / *hikiuke tesūryō* 引受け手数料 underwriting fee, underwriting spread

hi-kōkai kabushiki 非公開株式 non-public stock, private stock

himoku 費目 item of expenditure

***hinpaku 品薄** misreading for *shinausu* 品薄

hippaku 逼迫 tightness, stringency
Kinyū ga hippaku shite iru 金融が逼迫している The money market is

stringent. Money is tight / *hippaku-ji* 逼迫時 time of financial stringency

hiritsu 比率 ratio
toza hiritsu 当座比率 quick ratio, acid test ratio, quick assets ratio

hi-sanka-teki 非参加的 non-participating
hi-sanka-teki yūsen kabushiki 非参加的優先株式 non-participating preferred stock

hi-tōroku shōken 非登録証券 unregistered security
c.f. *tōroku shōken* 登録証券 registered security

hiyō 費用 expense

*hogō 歩合 misreading for *buai* 歩合

hōjin 法人 (in law) 'a juridical person', a corporation

kōeki hōjin 公益法人 non-profit foundation, public utilities corporation

hojo-kin 補助金 subsidy

hōkatsu 包括 comprehensive
hōkatsu shin'yō hoken 包括信用保険 blanket fidelity bonds

hoken 保険 insurance, assurance
kin'yū hoken 金融保険 investment trust and insurance (as a category of equities) / *seimei hoken* 生命保険 life assurance (sometimes shortened to *seiho* 生保) / *shin'yō hoken* 信用保険 fidelity bond / *songai hoken* 損害保険 non-life insurance / *hoken burōkā* 保険ブローカー insurance broker

hōkokusho 報告書 report
kigyō hōkokusho 企業報告書 company report

Honkon ホンコン Hong Kong
Honkon-doru ホンコン・ドル Hong Kong dollar

honnin 本人 a principal (in a transaction)

29

honrai-teki 本来的 intrinsic
honrai-teki kachi 本来的価値 intrinsic value, investment value

honzon 本尊 leader of a group of items
uri honzon 売り本尊 leader of short side

hosei yosan 補正予算 supplementary budget

hoshō 保証 assurance, guarantee
kakaku o hoshō suru 価格を保証する guarantee the price / *Teitō ni yori hoshō sarete ita kariire-kin no shiharai o kyōsei suru hōteki sochi* 抵当により保証されていた借入れ金の支払いを強制する法的措置 The legal process of enforcing payment of a debt secured by a mortgage / *hoshō sai* 保証債 guaranteed bond / *seifu hoshō sai* 政府保証債 government-guaranteed bond, contingent debt / *hoshō shōken* 保証証券 guaranteed issue

hoshu-teki 保守的 conservative

hoyū 保有 holding
hoyū daka 保有高 holding (lit. 'extent' or 'volume' 高 of 'holding' 保有) / *shōken hoyū daka* 証券保有高 dealer's position / *hoyū gaisai* 保有外債 foreign bonds on holdings, reserve external bonds / *hoyū shōken* 保有証券 securities holdings, investment portfolio

hyaku 百 100
FT hyakushu sōgō kabuka shisū FT百種総合株価指数 FT-SE 100 index

hyō 表 list, schedule, table
rimawari hyō 利回り表 yield book

hyōjun kinri 標準金利 standard rate (of interest)

hyōka kakaku 評価価格 evaluated amount, assessed value
hyōka son 評価損 evaluation loss

hyōshi 表紙 cover
hyōshi tegata 表紙手形 cover bill

hyōtei riritsu 評定利率 coupon rate

I

I- 伊 Italy
Itaria rira イタリア・リラ Italian lira / *Itaria 100 rira* イタリア100リラ
100 Italian lira

ichibu 一部 in some quarters, some (in a list)
*Ichibu seiho ga hoyū gaisai no kawase sason o kaihi suru tame doru-uri
ni deta* 一部生保が保有外債の為替差損を回避するためドル売りに出た
There was some dollar selling in life assurance stock in order to avoid exchange-
rate losses in foreign bonds

ichijun 一巡 cease to have an effect
lit. 'patrol', ' make a tour of' / *Kai ichijun-go, dareru (TSE)* 買い一巡後、だ
れる TSE: Dull, after brief buying

idō heikin sen 移動平均線 moving average

infure インフレ inflation
short for *infurēshion* インフレーション

iinkai 委員会 committee, commission
Shōken Torihiki Iinkai 証券取引委員会 US Securities and Exchange
Commission

ikkai niyari １カイ２ヤリ bid one, asked two;
one bid, offered two

ikkaku senkin 一獲千金 a killing (on the market)
lit. the *kaku* 獲 of 一獲 has a meaning of 'carry off' and 'snatch'. It has a
Japanese reading of *tsukamu* 獲む, 'to seize', 'to grasp'. Thus 一獲 means a
'snatching' etc. of the market. It is usually in combination with 千金 'a thousand
pieces of gold', and thus 一獲千金, lit. 'grabbing a thousand pieces of gold'
means variously, 'a killing on the market', 'making a fortune at a stroke', and
'getting rich in a single bound'

in 陰 shade, negative

in no kyoku 陰の極 rock-bottom. The situation in which a stock price has reached rock-bottom, lit. 'extreme' 極 of 'gloom' 陰. 陰 corresponds to the 'Yin' 陰 of the 'Yin and Yang' 陰陽 ('light and dark' or 'male and female') in Chinese philosophy

indekkusu インデックス index

indekkusu fuando インデックス・ファンド index fund / *koguchi no indekkusu-uri* 小口のインデックス売り small-lot index selling

infure hejji インフレ・ヘッジ hedging against inflation

inkamu fuando インカム・ファンド income fund

inkamu gen インカム・ゲン (also *inkamu gein* インカム・ゲイン) income gain

insaidā torihiki インサイダー取引 insider trading, insider dealing

ippan 一般 general

Kanzei Bōeki Ippan Kyōtei 関税貿易一般協定 GATT (General Agreement on Tariffs and Trade, generally referred to in Japanese as *Gatto* ガット) / *ippan jigyō sai* 一般事業債 general corporate bonds / *ippan kokyaku torihiki shijō* 一般顧客取引市場 outside market, retail market (lit. 'general client, public client' 一般顧客 'trading market' 取引市場 'trading market') / *ippan shisan* 一般資産 general assets / *ippan tōshika* 一般投資家 individual investor, the investing public

ippuku 一服 a lull

lit. 'a rest', it is also used in the sense of 'a dose' of medicine or a 'puff' of tobacco. Thus, *Ippuku shimashō ka* 一服しましょうか 'Shall we take a rest?', and *Ippuku ikaga desu ka* 一服いかがですか 'How about a cigarette?'

ison 依存 dependence

isondo 依存度 rate of independence / *yunyū isondo* 輸入依存度 rate of dependence on imports

itaku baibai 委託売買 brokerage, agency transaction

lit. 'trust, commission' 委託 'buying and selling' 売買 / *itaku hoshō-kin* 委託保証金 margin / *itaku hoshō-kin ritsu* 委託保証金率 margin requirements / *itaku tesuryō* 委託手数料 brokerage commission

ittei 一定 specified
ittei no manki o motsu shōsho ni yotte urazukerarete iru shihon 一定の満期を持つ証書によって裏付けられている資本 capital underwritten through certificates with specific maturity / *ittei kakaku* 一定価格 specified price

ittekoi いってこい 'see you here again' price movement
Used when a price returns to its original level within a day or other fixed period. いってこい, literally 'Go and come back' or 'we'll see you later', is a form of the greeting *Itte irasshai* 行っていらっしゃい said to a person leaving a house with the intention of coming back shortly

iyake 嫌気 dislike, disgust
Sono go wa kawase shijō no Ei-pondo nanchō o iyake shi, shijō wa yōsumi-kibun ga tsuyoi その後は為替市場の英ポンド軟調を嫌気し、市場は様子見気分が強い Traders tended to stay on the sidelines thereafter, discouraged by the weakening of the British pound

izon 依存 dependence (see *ison* 依存)

J

-jaku 弱 a little under
1,000-en-jaku 1000 円弱 a little under Yen 1,000

jakuden kiki 弱電機器 light electrical appliances
jakuden kabu 弱電株 short for *jakuden kiki kabu* 弱電機器株 light electrical appliances stock / *Jakuden kabu wa kai ga tsuzukazu yasuku nari...* 弱電株は買いが続かず安くなり... Light electrical appliances stocks ceased selling and fell in price...

jiai 地合 texture, weave
shikin yojō jiai 資金余剰地合 overall pattern of excess funds / *jichitai sai* 自治体債 issues in regard of a local, municipal or prefectural corporation / *chihō jichitai sai* 地方自治体債 regional issues

jigane 地金 gold bullion

jigyō 事業 business, enterprise, works
kokyō jigyō 公共事業 public utilities, public enterprise, public works enterprise / *jigyō sai* 事業債 corporate bonds / *ippan jigyō sai* 一般事業債 general corporate bonds

jika 時価 current price, market price, fair price
jika sōgaku 時価総額 total value at market price

jikihane ジキハネ *jikihane*-type bills in the bankers' acceptance (BA) market
Jikihane bills are issued by either domestic or foreign importers for the purpose of raising yen funds necessary for sight payments for imports

jikkō 実行 implementation
teitōken no jikkō 抵当権の実行 implementation of mortgage, foreclosure

jiko kabu 自己株 treasury stock
jiko kabushiki 自己株式 treasury stock / *jiko shihon* 自己資本 funds on hand, equities

jiri hin ジリ貧 sagging, gradual decline, tailspinning

jirijiri ジリジリ gradually, step-by-step
En wa 127-en 70-sen kinpen made jirijiri to ne o agete torihiki o shūryō shita 円は127円70銭近辺までジリジリと値を上げて取引を終了した The Yen gradually rose to close trading at around ¥127.70 (against the dollar)

jisseki 実績 actual results
This is, for the past fiscal year and before, as opposed to *mikomi* 見込み prospects for the current fiscal year, and *yosoku* 予測 for predictions for next fiscal year onwards

jisshitsu 実質 real
jisshitsu yokin 実質預金 real deposit

jiyū 自由 free, liberalized
jiyū bōeki 自由貿易 free trade / *jiyūka* 自由化 liberalization / *kakaku jiyūka* 価格自由化 price liberalization / *kome jiyūka* 米自由化 liberalization of rice /

jiyū kyōsō baibai shijō 自由競争売買市場 free auction market

*jōchi 上値 misreading for *uwane*

*jōdo 讓渡 misreading for *jōto*

jōgen 上限 upper limit
rieki ga yosō no jōgen datta no o ukete jōshō 利益が予想の上限だった
のを受けて上昇 the share price rose on the announcement that profits were at
the upper end of market expectations

jōhō 情報 information
kaisha naibu no jōhō 会社内部の情報 inside information / *jōhō kōkai* 情報
公開 disclosure

jōhō 上方 upwards
jōhō shūsei 上方修正 upward revision

jōi shōken 上位証券 senior issue

jōjō 上場 listing on a stock market
uraguchi jōjō 裏口上場 'backdoor listing' (achieved by a non-listed company
amalgamating with a listed company) / *jōjō haishi* 上場廃止 delisting / *jōjō
kabu* 上場株 listed stock / *jōjō kabushiki* 上場株式 listed stock / *jōjō kijun*
上場基準 listing requirements / *jōjō shinseisho* 上場申請書 application to
list / *jōjō shō ken* 上場証券 listed security / *hi-jōjō shōken* 非上場証券
unlisted security

jōken 条件 condition
kō-jōken 好条件 favourable market conditions

jōki 上期 first half (of fiscal year), interim
jōki kessan 上期決算 interim business results

jōmu 常務 also *jōmu torishimari yaku* 常務取締役 manag. dir.
see also *shachō* 社長 president / *fuku-shachō* 副社長 vice-president / *kaichō*
会長 chairman / *senmu* 専務 (also *senmu torishimairi yaku* 専務取締役) /
buchō 部長 divisional director / *kachō* 課長 sectional head

jōshō 上昇 rise, boost, upturn

bukka jōshō 物価上昇 price rises, rises in the cost of living / *kakaku jōshō* 価格上昇 price rise / *Kakaku jōshō wa kanwa sareta* 価格上昇は緩和された The rise in prices was kept at moderate levels

jōto 讓渡 transfer

kabushiki jōto 株式讓渡 assignment of certificate / *tochi daikin jōto teitō* 土地代金讓渡抵当 purchase money mortgage / *jōto shōsho* 讓渡証書 assignment certificate / *besshi no jōto shōsho* 別紙の讓渡証書 detached assignment, assignment separate from the certificate

jōyo 剰余 surplus, residue

jōyo kin 剰余金 surplus / *rieki jōyo kin* 利益剰余金 earned surplus

jūden kabu 重電株 heavy (duty) electrical machinery stock

short for *jūden kiki kabu* 重電機器株

juken 授権 authorization

juken kabushiki 授権株式 authorized stock / *juken shihon* 授権資本 authorized capital

jukyū 需給 supply and demand

the order of the Japanese is 需 'demand' and 給 'supply' / *shikin jukyū* 資金需給 supply and demand of funds

jun- 準 quasi-, semi-

jun-ote shōken kaisha 準大手証券会社 second-tier securities house

junbi kin 準備金 equity

shihon junbi kin 資本準備金 net worth, stockholders' equity / *junbi yokin* 準備預金 reserve deposits / *Yutanpo kōru mo shikin no dashite ga junbi yokin o tsumiageta tame, kitsume no torihiki datta* 有担保コールも預金の出手が準備預金を積み上げたため、きつ目の取引だった Trading in collateralled calls was fairly stringent due to the accumulation of reserve deposits by providers of funds

junkan 循環 circulation, rotation

shikin junkan 資金循環 flow of funds, flow of accounts

jūtaku 住宅 housing

kōteki jūtaku 公的住宅 public housing / *kōteki jū taku kensetsu shikin*

36

muke saiken 公的住宅建設資金向け債券 public housing agency bond

jutakusha 受託者 trustee

jūto 充当 appropriation, setting aside

juyō 需要 demand
kokunai juyō 国内需要 (often *naiju* 内需) domestic demand / *juyō kakudai* 需要拡大 expansion of demand / *juyō kyokyū* 需要供給 (also *jukyū* 需給) supply and demand / *juyō sha* 需要者 the demand sector, consuming industries, user / *Juyō sha ga neagari o mikoshite zaiko-gai ni hashitta* 需要者が値上がりを見越して在庫買いに走った The demand sector anticipated price rises and rushed to buy up stocks

K

kabā カバー to cover, to offset (a loss etc.)
see also *sōsai* 相殺 / *kabarejji* カバレッジ coverage

kabu 株 stock, share
The various meanings of *kabu* 株 are: (1) The stumps or roots of a felled tree (2) The cut-off remains of a plant with several stems (3) In Tokugawa Japan, rights monopolized by the members of a *kabu nakama* 株仲間, guilds formed by merchants in Edo, Kyoto and Osaka, with government licences. A kind of shareholders' union (4) In Tokugawa Japan, duties or offices, and family names, that could be bought or sold (5) A share, or a share certificate (6) Holdings (7) Status
Other meanings of 株 include 'convention', 'a normal practice', and 'a forte'. 株 is a hard-working word which appears to cover many of the meanings of the word 'stock' in English, including '(government) securities', the 'stem' or 'trunk of a tree', and ' family' or 'lineage' / *Kabu o kau* 株を買う means 'to invest in stocks' or 'to buy an interest in a business' / *Kabu o uru* 株を売る means 'to sell shares', or in the case of a doctor or lawyer, 'to sell one's business'.
株 is also a classifier for plants or trees, and also for shares. Thus, *take jukkabu* 竹十株 'ten stems of bamboo'; *Matsushita senkabu* 松下千株 'A thousand

shares in Matsushita' / Etymologically, *kabu* 蕪 'turnip' is closely related / *futsū kabu* 普通株 ordinary stock (UK), common stock (US) / *jiko kabu* 自己株 treasury stock / *jōjō kabu* 上場株 listed stock / *jōjō kabushiki* 上場株式 listed stock / *kagaku kabu* 化学株 chemical products stock (short for *kagaku seihin kabu* 化学製品株) / *kagaku seihin kabu* 化学製品株 chemical products stock / *kari kabu* 借り株 borrowed stock, stock loans / *kawase binkan kabu* 為替敏感株 exchange rate sensitive issues / *kinko kabu* 金庫株 treasury stock / *kinyū kabu* 金融株 finance stock / *kōbo kabu* 公募株 publicly subscribed share / *mizumashi kabu* 水増し株 a watered-down, diluted stock / *mizuwari kabu* 水割株 a watered stock / *mu-gakumen kabu* 無額面株 no-par stock / *ninki kabu* 人気株 active stock, star performer / *ōgata kabu* 大型株 large-capital stock (such as steel or shipbuilding stock) / *ryūtsū kabu* 流通株 distribution industry stock / *Ryūtsū kabu de takai mono ga medatta* 流通株で高いものが目立った High prices featured among distribution industry stock / *seichō kabu* 成長株 growth stock / *seimitsu kabu* 精密株 (short for *seimitsu kikai kabu* 精密機械株) precision instruments stock / *shinausu kabu* 品薄株 narrow-market / *tan'i kabu* 単位株 round lot, full lot / *teii kabu* 低位株 low-priced stock, lesser grade stock / *tekkō kabu* 鉄鋼株 steel industry stock / *teko kabu* テコ株 leverage stock / *yakuhin kabu* 薬品株 pharmaceuticals stock / *yūryō kabu* 優良株 blue chips / *zōsen kabu* 造船株 shipbuilding stock / *kabu atsume* 株集め accumulation of shares (see also *gyoku atsume* 玉集め)

kabuka 株価 a stock price, share price, quotation
kabuka o ki ni suru 株価を気にする be price-conscious about share prices / *heikin kabuka* 平均株価 average stock price / *tekisei kabuka han'i* 適正株価範囲 intrinsic range / *kabuka bōraku* 株価暴落 share crash, a heavy fall in shares prices / *kabuka heikin* 株価平均 price average / *kabuka kyasshu-furō hiritsu* 株価キャッシュ・フロー比率 price cash-flow ratio (PCR) / *kabuka' shisū* 株価指数 share index, stock price index (as in Financial Times *hyakushu kabuka shisū* ファイナンシャル・タイムズ百種株価指数 'FT 100-share Index') / *kabuka shūeki ritsu* 株価収益率 price earnings ratio (PER) / *kabuka sōsa* 株価操作 share manipulation

kabuken 株券 share certificate, stock certificate

kabunushi 株主 shareholder
kabunushishi sōkai 株主総会 shareholders' general meeting

kabushiki 株式 stock, share (of capital stock)

juken kabushiki 授権株式 authorized stock / *kihakkō kabushiki* 既発行株
式 outstanding stock (lit. 'already' 既 'issued' 発行 'stock' 株式) / *kōkai
kabushiki* 公開株式 publicly held stock / *meimoku gakumen kabushiki*
名目額面株式 nominal par value stock / *mi-hakkō kabushiki* 未発行株式 unissued stock / *mu-gakumen kabushiki* 無額面株式 non-par stock (see also 無
額面株) / *sankateki yūsen kabushiki* 参加的優先株式 participating preferred
stock / *sōhakkō kabushiki* 総発行株式 total issued stock / *teigakumen
kabushiki* 低額面株式 low par value stock / *yūsen kabushiki* 優先株式
preferred stock / *kabushiki hikiukeken* 株式引受権 subscription right /
kabushiki hakkōsha 株式発行者 issuer / *kabushiki jōto* 株式譲渡
assignment of certificate / *kabushiki kaisha* (also *kabushiki gaisha*) 株式会
社 business corporation, joint stock company, Co., Ltd / *kabushiki rimawari*
株式利回り dividend return / *kabushiki-sū* 株式数 number of shares /
kabushiki torihiki zei 株式取引税 transfer tax / *kabushiki tōrokunin* 株式
登録人 registrar of stock / *kabushiki tōshi shintaku* 株式投資信託 stock
investment trust

kachi 価値 value

genkin shisan kachi 現金資産価値 cash assets value / *honraiteki kachi* 本
来的価値 intrinsic value, investment value / *keizoku kigyō kachi* 継続企業価
値 going-concern value / *seisan kachi* 精算価値 break-up values, liquidation /
shisan kachi 資産価値 asset value

kachō 課長 sectional head

see also *shachō* 社長 president / *fuku-shachō* 副社長 vice-president / *kaichō*
会長 chairman / *senmu* 専務 (also *senmu torishimari yaku* 専務取締役)
executive director / *jōmu* 常務 (also *jōmu torishimari yaku* 常務取締役)
managing director / *buchō* 部長 divisional director

kagaku 化学 chemistry

kagaku kabu 化学株 chemical products stock (short for 化学製品株) / *kagaku
seihin kabu* 化学製品株 chemical products stock (also shortened to 化学株) /
kagaku sekiyu 化学石油 chemicals & petroleum (as a category of equities)

kagaku 価額 amount, value

hyōka kagaku 評価価額 assessed amount, assessed value / *kouri kagaku* 小売
価額 retail price

kahō 下方 downwards

kahō shūsei 下方修正 downward revision

kai 買い buying

kai chūmon 買い注文 bid / *kai yobine* 買い呼び値 bidding price, bid / *kai atsumeru* 買い集める to correct by purchase

kai 下位 junior

lit. 'subordinate', 'low-ranking' / *kai shōken* 下位証券 junior issue

kai 会 meeting, committee, association

sewanin kai 世話人会 (long-term government bond) facilitation committee

kaifuku 回復 recovery

keiki kaifuku 景気回復 economic recovery / *Zurekomu keiki kaifuku de gensan, zaiko chōsei kyōka e* ずれ込む景気回復で減産、在庫調整強化へ Reduced production and further inventory adjustment as recovery recedes

kaigai 海外 overseas

kaigai seisan 海外生産 (Japanese) production overseas / *kaigai shinshutsu* 海外進出 moving into a foreign market / *kaigai sōba* 海外相場 overseas markets

*kaigata 買方 misreading for *kaikata*

*kaigoshi 買い越し misreading for *kaikoshi*

kaihatsu 開発 development

kenkyū kaihatsu 研究開発 research and development (R&D) / *kaihatsu hi* 開発費 development expense

kaihi 回避 avoiding

Ichibu seiho ga hoyū gaisai no kawase sason o kaihi suru tame doru-uri ni deta 一部生保が保有外債の為替差損を回避するためドル売りに出た There was some dollar selling in life assurance stock in order to avoid exchange-rate losses in foreign bonds

kaihō 開放 opening up, the granting of access to a market

kin'yū shihon shijō no kaihō 金融資本市場の開放 opening up of capital financial markets

kaiin kaisha 会員会社 member firm (of the stock exchange)

kaiin ken 会員権 membership (of a stock exchange)

kaiireru 買い入れる purchase, buying, credit taking
see also *kainyū* 介入 / *Sumita Nichigin Sōsai no doru-gai kainyū o shisa suru hatsugen mo tetsudatte shōsha nado ga doru o kaiire...* 澄田日銀総裁のドル買い介入を示唆する発言も手伝って商社などがドルを買い入れ... The statement by Satoshi Sumita, Governor of the Bank of Japan, which hinted at dollar intervention by the Bank, induced trading houses and so on to purchase dollars...

kaiire shōkyaku 買い入れ償却 repayment by purchase

kaiisogi 買い急ぎ scurrying, over-ordering, scare-buying
lit. 'hurry' 急ぎ to 'buy' 買い

kaikaku 改革 reform
zeisei kaikaku 税制改革 tax reforms

kaikata 買方 buyer, a bull

kaikei 会計 accounts
kaikei kansa 会計監査 audit, auditing / *kaikei nendo* 会計年度 fiscal year. In contrast to *rekinen* 歴年 'calendar year'. Thus *1992-nendo* 1992年度 will be translated as FY 1992 or FY 1992/3, while *1992-nen* 1992年 will be translated as 'calendar 1992' or simply '1992'

kaikoshi 買い越し net buying

kaimochi 買い持ち long position

kaimodoshi 買い戻し repurchase, bear-covering, short-covering
Doitsu maruku ni taishite doru o kaimodosu ugoki ga deta tame, tai-en de mo doru-uri ga kōtai shita ドイツ・マルクに対してドルを買い戻す動きが出たため、対円でもドル売りが後退した Since there was the tendency to buy back the dollar against the German Mark, dollar-selling against the yen pulled back / *karauri no kaimodoshi* 空売りの買い戻し short covering

kainyū 介入 intervention, purchase
see also *kaiireru* 買い入れる / *Sumita Nichigin Sōsai no doru-gai kainyū o shisa suru hatsugen mo tetsudatte shōsha nado ga doru o kaiire...* 澄

田日銀総裁のドル買い介入を示唆する発言も手伝って商社などがドルを買い入れ... The statement by Satoshi Sumita, Governor of the Bank of Japan, which hinted at a dollar intervention by the Bank, induced trading houses and so on to purchase dollars... / *kyōchō kainyū* 協調介入 concerted intervention / *kainyū keikaikan* 介入警戒感 a fear of intervention / *Doitsu maruku wa kainyū keikaikan ga tsuyoku kougoki de 1 doru=1.4695-1.4705 maruku* ドイツ・マルクは介入警戒感が強く小動きで1ドル=1.4695-1.4705マルク The German Mark kept to a narrow range for fear of intervention and changed hands at 1.4695-1.4705 to the dollar

kaiope tegata 買いオペ手形 buying operation, bill, draft, paper
Short for *kai-operēshon tegata* 買いオペレーション手形

kairi 乖離 divergence, diversion

kaisha 会社 company, corporation
kaiin kaisha (also *kaiin gaisha*) 会員会社 member firm (of the stock exchange) / *kanren kaisha* (also *kanren gaisha*) 関連会社 affiliated company / *mujin kaisha* 無尽会社 mutual financing (loan) association, mutual financing (loan) business. The traditional type of financing institution (lit. 'inexhaustible' 無尽 'company' 会社) / *shintaku kaisha* (also *shintaku gaisha*) 信託会社 trust company / *tanshi kaisha* (also *tanshi gaisha*) 短資会社 short-term credit dealer, money market dealer / *kaisha naibu* 会社内部 inside a company / *kaisha naibu no jōhō* 会社内部の情報 inside information / *kaisha seiri* 会社整理 termination of a business (by the conversion of its assets into cash, lit. 'disposal' 整理 of a 'company' 会社) / *kaisha sōgo kan no kanjō* 会社相互間の勘定 inter-company accounts

kaishi 開始 commencement
tachiai kaishi 立会い開始 opening of market

kaishime 買占め cornering

kaite 買い手 client, customer, purchaser

kaiten 回転 turnover
kaiten akinai 回転商い over-trading

kaitori 買い取り buy, purchase, takeover

kaitsuke 買い付け buy, buy in, purchase

kaitsuke no honya 買い付けの本屋 one's favourite bookshop / *kōkai kaitsuke* 公開買い付け takeover bid, tender offer / *kaitsuke chū mon* 買い付け注文 buying order

kaizen 改善 improvement

hyōjun ninshō tetsuzuki no kaizen 標準認証手続きの改善 improvement in standards and certification procedures

kajū heikin 荷重平均 weighted average

kakaku 価格 price, value

ittei kakaku 一定価格 specified price / *kakaku o hoshō suru* 価格を保証する guarantee the price / *... kakaku de nyūsatsu suru* ...価格で入札する bid at such-and-such (...) a price / *kisai kakaku* 記載価格 stated value, declared value / *konyū kakaku* 購入価格 purchase price / *kōshi kakaku* 行使価格 price in force / *kōtei kakaku* 公定価格 official price / *nyūsatsu kakaku* 入札価格 bidding price, price bid / *sōba kakaku* 相場価格 market price / *kakaku jōshō* 価格上昇 price rise

kakekin 掛金 instalment, fixed amount

sōgo kakekin 相互掛金 instalment savings

kakki 活気 vigour

kakki aru shijō 活気ある市場 brisk market

kakudai 拡大 expansion

Bei-bōeki kakudai 米貿易拡大 expansion in US trade / *bōeki akaji kakudai* 貿易赤字拡大 rising trade deficit (lit. 'trade' 貿易 'red figures' 赤字 'expansion' 拡大) / *bōeki kuroji kakudai* 貿易黒字拡大 rising trade surplus (lit. 'trade' 貿易 'black figures' 黒字 'expansion' 拡大) / *juyō kakudai* 需要拡大 expansion in demand / *naiju kakudai* 内需拡大 expansion of the domestic market (lit.'domestic' *naikoku* 内国 'demand' 需要 'expansion' 拡大)

kakuritsu 確率 probability

kakusa 格差 differential

ōpun kinri to tegata rēto no kakusa ga shukushō shite kita オープン金利と手形レートの格差が縮小してきた Differentials between open rates and bill rates have narrowed

kakutei 確定 fixed, certain
kakutei ritsuki shōken 確定利付き証券 fixed-interest security

kakutoku 獲得 earn, acquire
gaika kakutoku 外貨獲得 earning foreign currency

kakuzuke 格付け credit rating, grading

kami 紙 paper
sen'i kami 繊維紙 textiles & paper (as a category of equities)

Kanada カナダ Canada
Kanada-doru カナダ・ドル Canadian dollar

kanendo 過年度 preceding fiscal year

kanetsu 過熱 hot
lit. 'super hot'. The term is borrowed from industrial terminology: for example, *kanetsu suijōki* 過熱水蒸気 'superheated steam' / *89-nen wa kanetsu kara antei e mukau odoriba to natta to ieru.* 89年は過熱から安定へ向かう踊り場になったと言える 1989 marked the transition from a period of overheating to a period of stability / *kanetsu ninki no shinkabu* 過熱人気の新株 hot issue

kanezumari 金詰まり tightness of money, monetary stringency

kanji 幹事 manager
hikiuke gyōsha kanji 引受業者幹事 syndicate manager / *hikiuke kanji tesuryō* 引受幹事手数料 managing fee / *kanji tesuryō* 幹事手数料 managing fee

kanjō 勘定 account
kaisha sōgo kan no kanjō 会社相互間の勘定 inter-company accounts / *shihon kanjō* 資本勘定 net worth, stockholders' equity / *son'eki kanjō* 損益勘定 profit and loss statement, income account

Kankoku 韓国 Republic of Korea; ROK; South Korea
Kankoku uon 韓国ウォン the Korean dollar

*kanmi zairyō 甘味材料 misreading for *amami zairyō*

kanren 関連 connection, relation, association
kanren kaisha (also *kanren gaisha*) 関連会社 affiliated company

kanrinin 管理人 custodian

kanryū 還流 recycling, channelling back
Shikin jukyū wa Nichigin-ken no kanryū nado de 2,100-oku-en no yojō 資金需給は日銀券の還流などで2100億円の余剰 The supply and demand of funds reached a surplus of ¥210bn with the recycling of Bank of Japan bonds

kansa 監査 inspection, audit
kaikei kansa 会計監査 auditing, an audit / *kansa-zumi* 監査済み after audit

kansan 閑散 quiet, thin

kansan 換算 convert
en kansan de 円換算で expressed in yen / *nenritsu kansan de* 年率換算で on an annualized basis

kanshi 監視 monitoring
also *monitaringu* モニタリング

kanwa 緩和 easing, moderation
Kakaku jōshō wa kanwa sareta 価格上昇は緩和された The rises in prices were kept at moderate levels

kanzai 管財 receivership
kanzai-nin 管財人 receiver

kanzei 関税 customs, custom duty, tariff
sōsai kanzei 相殺関税 compensation duties, countervailing duties, countervailing tariff / *kanzei hikisage* 関税引下げ tariff reductions / *Kanzei Bōeki Ippan Kyōtei* 関税貿易一般協定 GATT (General Agreement on Tariffs and Trade, referred to more usually as *Gatto* ガット)

kappatsu 活発 brisk, vigorous, lively
Tegata torihiki wa Nichigin ope-bun o nozoku baibai-daka ga 4,500-oku-en ni haramu kappatsu na akinai to natta 手形取引は日銀オペ分を

除く売買高が4,500億円にはらむ活発な商いとなった There was lively trading in bills, amounting to a massive turnover of ¥450bn, excluding the proportion of the Bank of Japan's operation bills

kappu tōshi 割賦投資 instalment, investment
see also *doru heikin hō* ドル平均法

kara torihiki 空取引 washed sales, fictitious transaction

*karaku 下落 misreading for *geraku*

karauri 空売り short sale, short selling
karauri no kaimodoshi 空売りの買い戻し short covering

*karigata 借方 misreading for *karikata*

kariire 借入 borrowing, credit-taking
kariire-gaku 借入額 a debt (worth ¥...) / *kariire-kin* 借入金 debt, loan, broker's loan, borrowed money / *kariire saki* 借入先 channel for raising funds / *kariire shōsho* 借入証書 loan certificate / *kariire-zan* 借入残 debit balance

kari kabu 借株 borrowed stock, stock loans

karikae 借換え conversion, refunding, reborrowing
karikae-sai 借換え債 roll-over bonds, refunding bonds

karikata 借方 debtor

kasegi 稼ぎ profit-taking
nezaya kasegi 値ザヤ稼ぎ profit-taking arbitrage transactions

kashidashi 貸出し loan, advance

kashikata 貸方 creditor
kashikata zandaka 貸方残高 credit balance

kashitsuke 貸付け loan
Chōtanki no saikensha yori kashitsukerareta shihon 長短期の債権者より貸付られた資本 Capital financed by long- and short-term creditors / *kashitsuke-kin* 貸付け金 loan / *mutanpo kashitsuke kin* 無担保貸付け金

unsecured loan / *kashitsuke shintaku* 貸付け信託 loan trust

kawarazu 変わらず unchanged

kawase 為替 exchange, exchange rate

Goba ni hairu to, kawase ga 1-doru=127en dai zenpan de kougoki to nari... 後場に入ると、為替が1ドル=127円台前半で小動きとなり... In the afternoon session, the exchange rate moved slightly to the lower regions of $1= ¥127... / *gaikoku kawase shijō* 外国為替市場 foreign exchange (forex) market / *nami-kawase* 並為替 ordinary remittance / *kawase binkan kabu* 為替敏感株 exchange rate-sensitive issues / *kawase risuku* 為替リスク risks arising from exchange rate fluctuations / *kawase risuku o bunsan suru* 為替リスクを分散する spread the risk arising from currency fluctuations / *kawase sason* 為替差損 exchange differentials, exchange losses / *hoyū gaisai no kawase sason o kaihi suru tame no doru-uri ni deru* 保有外資の為替差損を回避するためのドル売りに出る sell dollars in order to avoid losses from the differences in quotations on reserve external bonds / *kawase tegata* 為替手形 bill of exchange

kazei 課税 imposition of taxes, duty, levy

kehai 気配 tone of the market

kehai-chi 気配値 quotation

kehai-chi o agete yoritsuita 気配値を上げて寄付いた the market opened amid bid-only quotations / *kehai-chi o sagete yoritsuita* 気配値を下げて寄付いた the market opened amid asked-only quotations

kei 計 total (in table)

keiei 経営 management, operation, proprietorship

kojin keiei 個人経営 sole proprietorship / *kyōdō keiei* 共同経営 joint management, partnership / *keiei-ken* 経営権 management right, franchise right / *keiei-ken shihai* 経営権支配 takeover (lit. 'control' 支配 of 'management right' 経営権)

keiji ban 掲示板 the quotation board of the New York Stock Exchange, and by extension, a nickname for the Exchange itself

keijō rieki 経常利益 recurring profits, pre-tax profits

keika 経過 passage
toki no keika 時の経過 passage of time / *keika rishi* 経過利子 accrued interest

keiki 景気 market conditions, market tone, business, liveliness
The very basic usages of this term are *keiki ga ii* 景気がいい 'Times are good' and *keiki ga warui* 景気が悪い 'Times are bad.' By extension: *keiki no ii hito* 景気のいい人 'lively-looking person'/ *keiki no ii hanashi* 景気のいい話 'get-rich quick story'/ *keiki no ii ongaku* 景気のいい音楽 'lively tune' / *keiki kaifuku* 景気回復 economic recovery / *zurekomu keiki kaifuku de gensan, zaiko chōsei kyōka e* ずれ込む景気回復で減産、在庫調整強化へ reduced production and further inventory adjustment as recovery recedes / *keiki kōtai* 景気後退 recession

keisan 計算 calculation

keisansho 計算書 statement
son'eki keisansho 損益計算書 income statement

keisu 係数 coefficient
sōkan keisu 相関係数 correlation coefficient / *kinri to kabuka no sōkan keisū* 金利と株価の相関係数 the correlation coefficient between interest rates and share prices

keiyaku 契約 contract, agreement, bargain
shintaku keiyaku 信託契約 indenture, deeds of trust / *keiyakusho* 契約書 contract, agreement, bargain (on paper) / *shintaku keiyakusho* 信託契約書 indenture, deeds of trust

keizai 経済 economy
Keizai Kikaku Chō 経済企画庁 Economic Planning Agency (EPA) / *keizai taisaku* 経済対策 economic measures / *sōgō keizai taisaku* 総合経済対策 comprehensive economic measures, package of emergency economic measures

keizoku 継続 continuation
Nichigin wa kijitsu no kita kai-ope-tegata sanzen-oku en no uchi nisen-oku en o keizoku shi 日銀は期日の来た買オペ手形三千億円のうち二千億円を継続し The Bank of Japan continued with ¥200bn of the ¥300bn-worth of buying operations bills which had reached maturity / *keizoku kigyō kachi* 継続

企業価値 going-concern value

ken 券 bond
Nichigin-ken 日銀券 Bank of Japan bond

kenchō 堅調 steady, firm solid
also *shikkari* しっかり) / *Tekkō , zōsen nado ōgata kabu ga kenchō de, kikai, kensetsu kabu mo shikkari...* 鉄鋼、造船など大型株が堅調で、機械、建設株もしっかり… Steel, shipbuilding and other large-capital stock were firm, as were machinery and construction stock

kenkyū 研究 research
kenkyū kaihatsu 研究開発 R&D (research and development)

kenri 権利 right
kenri gimu 権利義務 rights and duties (of a company, trustee, or a bondholder)

kenri ochi 権利落ち rights off
kenri shōsho 権利証書 warrant (stock purchase warrant) / *kenri-tsuki* 権利付き rights on, with warrants

kensetsu 建設 construction
kōteki jūtaku kensetsu shikin muke saiken 公的住宅資金向け債券 public housing agency bond / *kensetsu kabu* 建設株 construction stock

kessai 決裁 approval
Nichigin wa kijitsu o mukaeta kai-ope tegata yon-sen-oku-en no uchi ni-sen oku-en o kessai shite shikin o kyūshū 日銀は期日を迎えた買オペ手形 4 千億円のうち 2 千億円を決裁して資金を吸収 The bank of Japan approved the absorption of ¥20 billion out of a total of ¥40 billion in buying operation bills which had reached maturity

kessai 決済 liquidation, settlement, closing a transaction
see *kyūshū* 吸収 / *kessai o okonau* 決済を行なう conduct a settlement / *kessai tetsuzuki* 決済手続き settlement procedure / *kessai-bi* 決済日 settlement date

kessan 決算 business results, settlement of accounts
kessan no happyō 決算の発表 announcement of business results / *kō -kessan* 好決算 good business results

ki 期 (financial) term
1994-nen 3-gatsu-ki 1994年3月期 FY93 ending March 1994

kichō 基調 basic tone, basic trend, keynote
Shijō wa uri kichō de shūshi shita 市場は売り基調で終始した The market maintained an underlying bearish tone throughout the day / *kichō enzetsu* 基調演説 keynote speech

kigen 期限 due period
kigen ga kuru 期限が来る fall due / *mu-kigen* 無期限 unlimited, open / *mu-kigen chūmon* 無期限注文 open order

kigyō 企業 company, enterprise, corporation
chūshō kigyō 中小企業 small and medium enterprises / *keizoku kigyō* 継続企業 going concern / *keizoku kigyō kachi* 継続企業価値 going-concern value / *kigyō gōben* 企業合弁 (also *gōben* 合弁) merger, consolidation / *kigyō hōkokusho* 企業報告書 company report

ki-hakkō kabushiki 既発行株式 outstanding stock
lit. 'already' 既 'issued' 発行 'stock' 株式

kihakuka 希薄化 dilution

kijitsu 期日 fixed date, a term
kijitsu o mukaeta kai-ope tegata 期日を迎えた買オペ手形 operation bills which have reached maturity / *kōshi kijitsu* 行使期日 the date of completion e.g. of a call loan

kijun 基準 standard, criterion, benchmark, guideline
jōjō kijun 上場基準 listing requirements / *kijun ninshō seido* 基準認証制度 system of standards and certification / *kijun ninshō tetsuzuki no kaizen* 基準認証手続きの改善 improvements in standards and certification procedures / *kijun-bi* 基準日 base date

kikai 機械 machinery
as a category of equities / *kikai kabu* 機械株 machinery stock

kikaku 企画 planning
Keizai Kikaku Chō 経済企画庁 Economic Planning Agency (EPA)

kikan 期間 period, term
taiki kikan 待機期間 cooling-off period, waiting period / *kikan-betsu rimawari* 期間別利回り yield curve (lit. 'yield' 利回り 'by', 'according to' 別 'term' 期間)

kikan 機関 institution, organization
kōkyō kikan 公共機関 public issuers / *kikan tōshika* 機関投資家 institutional investors / *kikan tōshika torihiki* 機関投資家取引 trading by institutional investors

kiken 危険 risk, danger

kikinzoku 貴金属 precious metals
i.e. gold, platinum, silver

kimei 記名 register
kimei-sai 記名債 registered bond

kin 金 gold
kinjigane 金地金 gold bullion, gold ingot (lit. 地金 is 'ingot', 'ground metal') (*Jigane o awarasu* 地金を表す 'To show one's true colours') / *kin jigane tentō kakaku (tai-kokyaku - 1guramu)* 金地金店頭価格 (対顧客—1グラム) Gold bullion OTC price (customer price per gramme)

kingaku 金額 value
kingaku bēsu de 金額ベースで in terms of value

kingin 金銀 gold and silver
kingin hika 金銀比価 parity of gold and silver

kinko kabu 金庫株 treasury stock
also *jiko kabu* 自己株

Kinko 金庫 refers to a 'safe' in a bank, an office or the home
Here, however, it refers to 'financial bank' *kin'yū kinko* 金融金庫

kinkyū 緊急 emergency
kinkyū keizai taisaku 緊急経済対策 emergency economic measures / *kinkyū yunyū seigen* 緊急輸入制限 safeguards (lit. 'emergency' 緊急 'imports' 輸入 'limits' 制限)

kinpen 近辺 region
En wa 127-en 70-sen kinpen made jirijiri to ne o agete torihiki o shūryō shita 円は127円70銭近辺までジリジリと値を上げて取引を終了した The yen rose gradually to close trading at around ¥127.70 against the dollar

kinri 金利 interest, interest rate
Bei-kinri 米金利 American interest rates / *Bei-kinri sakidaka-kan no kōtai to Bei-bōeki akaji kakudai no omowaku kara doru-uri ga fueta* 米金利先高感の後退と米貿易赤字拡大の思惑からドル売りが増えた There was increased selling of dollars because of lower expectation of a rise in US interest rates and anticipation of an increase in the US trade deficit / *hyōjun kinri* 標準金利 standard rate of interest / *kō-kinri* 高金利 high interest rates / *ōpun kinri* オープン金利 open rates / *shiharai kinri* 支払い金利 interest on payments / *Kinri Chōsei Shingikai* 金利調整審議会 Interest Adjustment Council / *kinri sakidaka kan* 金利先高感 anticipation of a rise in interest rates

kinsen 金銭 money, cash
tokutei kinsen shintaku 特定金銭信託 special purpose trust / *kinsen shintaku* 金銭信託 ordinary money trusts, money in trust / *kinsenteki* 金銭的 monetary

kin'yū 金融 financing
kin'yū chōtatsu 金融調達 financing, procurement of finance / *kin'yū no hikishime* 金融の引き締め financial / monetary restraint, credit squeeze / *kin'yū hippakuji* 金融逼迫時 time of financial / monetary stringency, time of tightening financial positions / *kin'yū hoken* 金融保険 investment trusts and insurance (as a category of equities) / *kin'yū kabu* 金融株 financial stock / *kin'yū sai* 金融債 bank bond, bank debenture / *ritsuki kin'yū sai* 利付金融債 coupon bank debenture, interest-bearing bank debenture / *waribiki kin'yū sai* 割引金融債 discount bank debenture / *kin'yū shihon* 金融資本 financial capital / *kin'yū shihon shijō no kaihō* 金融資本市場の開放 liberalization of financial capital markets / *kin'yū shōhin* 金融商品 financial instrument

kinzoku 金属 metal
tekkō kinzoku 鉄鋼金属 steel & metals (as a category of equities)

kiochi 期落ち maturity
Tegata torihiki wa teichō de, kiochi 2,000-oku-en ni taishite Nichigin ope-bun o nozoku baibai-daka wa yaku-600-oku-en ni todomatta 手形取引は低調で、期落ち2000億円に対して日銀オペ分を除く売買高は約600億

円に留まった Bill trading was thin, and the volume of this trading, excluding BoJ operations, was only ¥60bn, as opposed to ¥200bn expected at maturity

kirisage 切り下げ devaluation

kisai 起債 float (a loan), issued (bonds)
kisai-kai 起債会 bond issue committee, underwriters' association

kisai 記載 stated, mentioned, published
kisai kakaku 記載価格 declared value, stated value

kisei 規制 regulation
Kyoninka ya kisei nado, doko made seifu ga kan'yo suru no ka no rūru o hakkiri sase, takoku-kan de chōsei shite takoku no shisutemu o chōwa sasete iku 許認可や規則など、どこまで政府が関与するのかのルールをはっきりさせ、多国間で調整して多国のシステムを調和させて行く To clarify the rules as to how far Government will take part in certification and regulation, and to harmonize various countries' systems through international cooperation

kisoku 規則 rules
kōsei torihiki kisoku 公正取引規則 rules for fair conduct (lit. 'fair' 公正 'trading' 取引 'rules' 規則)

kitei 規定 provisions, regulations, rules
kitei o seiritsu saseru 規定を成立させる formulate rules

kitsume きつめ fairly stringent
Yūtanpo kōru mo shikin no dashite ga junbi yokin o tsumiageta tame, kitsume no torihiki datta 有担保コールも資金の出し手が準備預金を積み上げたため、きつめの取引だった Trading in collateralled calls was fairly stringent due to the accumulation of reserve deposits on the part of providers of funds

kōbo 公募 public offering, public placing, public subscription
kōbo kabu 公募株 publicly subscribed share

kōeki 公益 public good
kōeki hojin 公益法人 non-profit foundation, public utilities corporation

kōfu 交付 delivery, grant, service
mushō kōfu 無償交付 free distribution, stock dividend

kōgai 公害 pollution
kōgai bōshi 公害防止 pollution prevention / *kōgai bōshi shisetsu muke saiken* 公害防止施設向け債券 pollution control bonds

kogaisha 子会社 subsidiary company

kogitte 小切手 cheque

koguchi 小口 small-lot
koguchi no indekkusu-uri 小口のインデックス売り small-lot index selling

kōgyō 鉱業 mining
suisan kōgyō 水産鉱業 fisheries & mining (as a category of equities)

kohaba 小幅 small-scale
kohaba zokushin 小幅続伸 slight continued rise

kojin 個人 individual person
kojin keiei 個人経営 sole proprietorship

kō-jōken 好条件 favourable market conditions

kōkai 公開 public
kōkai kabushiki 公開株式 publicly held stock / *kōkai kaitsuke* 公開買付け take-over bid, tender offer

kōkan 好感 good feeling, being bolstered by
Zenjitsu no Nyū Yōku sōba ga shijō saikō ne o kōshin shite hiketa no o kōkan shite... 前日のニューヨーク相場が史上最高値を更新して引けたのを好感して... Bolstered by another record high in New York the previous day...

kōkansho (also **kōkanjo**) **交換所** exchange
tegata kōkansho (also *tegata kōkanjo*) 手形交換所 clearing house

kōkennin 後見人 guardian

kō-kessan 好決算 good business results

kōki 後期 second half (of fiscal year)

kō-kinri 高金利 high interest rates

kokuei 国営 state-run
kokuei kigyō 国営企業 state-run business

kokumin 国民 nation
kokumin sōseisan 国民総生産 GNP

kokunai 国内 domestic
kokunai juyō 国内需要 domestic demand (often *naiju* 内需)

kokusai 国際 international
kokusai shisan un'yō 国際資産運用 international asset management /
Kokusai Tsuka Kikin 国際通貨基金 International Monetary Fund (IMF)

kokusai 国債 government bond
tanki kokusai 短期国債 short-term government bonds / *tokurei kokusai* 特例
国債 special bond / *waribiki kokusai* 割引国債 discount government bond

kokyaku 顧客 a client
ippan kokyaku torihiki shijō 一般顧客取引市場 outside market, retail
market

kōkyō 公共 public
kōkyō jigyō 公共事業 public works projects, public utilities projects / *kōkyō
kikan* 公共機関 public issuers

komāsharu pēpā コマーシャル・ペーパー commercial paper

kome 米 rice
kome jiyūka 米自由化 liberalization of rice

kōmoku 項目 item
rinji son'eki kōmoku 臨時損益項目 non-recurrent item

komon 顧問 adviser
komongyō 顧問業 advisory business, advisory service / *tōshi komongyō* 投資
顧問業 investment advisory service

kōnin 公認 public, chartered
kōnin shōken anarisuto 公認証券アナリスト chartered financial analyst

kōnyū 購入 purchase
kōnyū kakaku 購入価格 purchase price

kōri 高利 high interest
kōri-sai 高利債 high interest bond / *kō-rimawari* 高利回り good yield, high
rate of income

kōritsu 効率 efficiency
kōritsu-teki 効率的 efficient / *kōritsu-teki shijō* 効率的市場 efficient
market

kōru コール call loan, money on call
*Yū-tanpo kōru mo shikin no dashite ga junbi yokin o tsumiageta tame,
kitsume no torihiki datta* 有担保コールも資金の出し手が準備預金を積み
上げたため、きつめの取引だったTrading in collateralled calls was fairly
stringent due to the accumulation of reserve deposits on the part of providers of
funds / *Shikin yojō jiai datta ga, kōru mujōken-mono rēto wa
zenshūmatsu-hi-kawarazu no 4% (dashite) ni sueokareta* 資金余剰地合
だったが、コール無条件もののレートは前週末比変わらずの4%(出し手)に
据え置かれたThere was a general excess of funds, but the rate for unconditional
call loans was 4.0% (selling), unchanged from the previous weekend, and
therefore deferred / *kōru opushion* コール・オプション call option / *...o
taishō to suru kōru opushion, putto-opushion* ... を対象とするコール・
オプション、プット・オプション call options and put options on ...

kōsai 公債 civil issues

kōsei 構成 composition, structure, proportion
as in, for example, the proportion of the rare earths market occupied by China.
Usually, the bottom line of the column of figures will add up to 100 / *shihon
kōsei* 資本構成 capital composition, capital structure

kōsei 公正 fair
kōsei torihiki 公正取引 fair trading / *kōsei torihiki kisoku* 公正取引規則
rules for fair conduct (lit. 'fair' 公正 'trading' 取引 'rules' 規則)

kōsha-sai 公社債 public and corporate bonds

also: government bonds and corporate debentures / *Kōsha-Sai Hikiuke Kyōkai* 公社債引受協会 Bond Underwriters Association / *Kōsha-sai tōshi shintaku* 公社債投資信託 bond investment trust, open-ended bond investment trust

kōshi 行使 enforce, exercise, implement

opushion kōshi オプション行使 implementation of a call loan / *kōshi kakaku* 行使価格 the price in force / *kōshi kijitsu* 行使期日 date of completion of call loan

kōshin 更新 renew

Zenjitsu no Nyū Yōku sōba ga shijō saikō ne o kōshin shite hiketa no o kōkan shite... 前日のニューヨーク相場が史上最高値を更新して引けたのを好感して... Bolstered by another record high in New York the previous day...

kō-shūeki 高収益 fast profits, high profits

kōshūeki o ageru 高収益を上げる to make fast profits

kō-suijun 高水準 high level

kōtai 後退 withdrawal, pull-back

Doitsu maruku ni tai-shite doru o kaimodosu ugoki ga deta tame, tai-en de mo doru-uri ga kōtai shita ドイツ・マルクに対してドルを買い戻す動きが出たため、対円でもドル売りが後退した Since there was a trend to buy back dollars against the German mark, traders pulled back in their selling of the dollar against the yen / *keiki kōtai* 景気後退 recession

kotei 固定 fixed

yūkei kotei shisan 有形固定資産 tangible fixed assets / *kotei-hi* 固定費 fixed cost, fixed charge / *kotei shisan* 固定資産 fixed assets, capital assets / *kotei shisan baikyaku* 固定資産売却 sale of capital assets / *kotei tesuryō* 固定手数料 fixed commission

kōtei 公定 official, legal, prescribed

kōtei buai 公定歩合 official discount rate (ODR) / *kōtei kakaku* 公定価格 official price

kōteki 公的 public

kōteki jūtaku 公的住宅 public housing / *Kōteki jūtaku kensetsu shikin muke saiken* 公的住宅建設資金向け債券 public housing agency bonds / *kōteki shisan* 公的資産 public assets / *Zenba wa kōteki shisan, tōshi*

57

shintaku ga ōgata kabu ni kai o ire shikkari shita tenkai datta ga... 前場
は公的資産、投資信託が大型株に買いを入れしゃっかりした展開だった
が... The morning session showed a hiccup in buying large-capital stock by public
assets and investment trusts, but...

kougoki 小動き movement within a narrow range, slow movement, slight movement
Yokka no Rondon gaikoku kawase shijō no en-sōba wa kougoki 4日の
ロンドン外国為替市場の円相場は小動き On the London forex market of 4
August the dollar weakened against the yen / *Goba ni hairu to, kawase ga 1-
doru = 127-en-dai zenpan de kougoki to nari...* 後場に入ると、為替が1
ドル＝127円台前半で小動きとなり... In the after session, the exchange rate
moved slightly to the lower reaches of $1 =¥127...

kouri 小売 retail
kouri kagaku 小売価格 retail price

koyasui 小安い soft, easy, weak
koyasuku hiketa 小安く引けた finished weak

kōza 口座 account
shōken torihiki kōza 証券取引口座 account in securities / *sōgō kōza* 総合口
座 general accounts

kōzō 構造 structure
kōzō chōsei 構造調整 structural adjustment

kūdōka 空洞化 hollowing-out
as when an industry shifts to production overseas, leaving a vacuum in the
domestic industry

kuitsubusu 食い潰す make inroads into

kumiai 組合 union
pūru-sei kumiai sōsa プール制組合操作 pool operation / *shinyō kumiai*
信用組合 trust fund

kurinobe 操り延べ carrying over, deferment, postponement

kuroji 黒字 surplus

lit. 'black' 黒 'figures' 字 'in the black' / *bōeki kuroji* 貿易黒字 trade surplus / *bōeki kuroji kakudai* 貿易黒字拡大 rise in trade surplus (lit. expansion in trade surplus)

kyapitaru gein キャピタル・ゲイン capital gains

kyasshu-furō キャッシュ・フロー cash-flow
kyasshu-furō hiritsu キャッシュ・フロー比率 cash flow ratio / *kabuka kyasshu-furō ritsu* 株価キャッシュ・フロー率 price cash flow ratio for stock

-kyō 強 a little over
Tegata torihiki wa Nichigin-ope o nozoite 1,200-oku-en kyō 手形取引は日銀オペを除いて1200億円強 Trading in bills, with the exception of bills operated by the BoJ, amounted to a little over ¥120 billion

kyōchō 協調 cooperation
kyōchō kainyū 協調介入 concerted intervention

kyōdō 共同 joint
kyōdō keiei 共同経営 joint management, partnership

kyoka 許可 admission
aru meigara o torihikijo de baibai suru koto no kyoka ある銘柄を取引所で売買することの許可 admission of a security to be traded on the stock exchange

kyōka 強化 reinforcement
EC wa tai-Nichi tsūshō seisaku o kyōka shite iru ECは対日通商政策を強化している The EC is reinforcing its trade policy towards Japan / *zurekomu keiki kaifuku de gensan, zaiko chōsei kyōka e* ずれ込む景気回復で減産、在庫調整強化へ reduced production and further inventory adjustment as recovery recedes

kyōkai 協会 association
Kōsha-sai Hikiuke Kyōkai 公社債引受協会 Bond Underwriters Association

kyōkyū 供給 supply
juyō kyōkyū 需要供給 supply and demand / *tsūka kyōkyū* 通貨供給 money supply

59

kyonin 許認 certification
kyoninka 許認化 increased certification / *Kyoninka ya kisei nado, doko made seifu ga kan'yo suru no ka no rūru o hakkiri sase, takoku-kan de chōsei shite takoku no shisutemu o chōwa sasete iku* 許認可や規制など、どこまで政府が関与するのかのルールをはっきりさせ、多国間で調整して多国のシステムを調和させて行く To clarify the rules as to how far Government will take part in certification and regulation, and to harmonize various countries' systems through international cooperation

kyōran 狂乱 frenzy
kyōran bukka 狂乱物価 spiralling inflation, inflation out of control

kyōsō 競争 competition, rivalry
kyōsō baibai 競争売買 auction (lit. 'competition' 競争 'buying and selling' 売買, see also *seri baibai* 競り売買) *kyōsō baibai shijō* 競争売買市場 auction market / *jiyū kyōsō baibai shijō* 自由競争売買市場 free auction market / *kyōsō nyūsatsu* 競争入札 competitive bidding

kyōtei 協定 agreement, convention
Kanzei Bōeki Ippan Kyōtei 関税貿易一般協定 GATT (General Agreement on Tariffs and Trade) The agreement is referred to in Japanese more usually as *Gatto,* ガット

kyōtsū 共通 common
kyōtsū tsūshō seisaku 共通通商政策 common trade policy

kyūgen 急減 rapid decline, sharp fall
kyū-hanraku 急反落 sharp set-back, strong reaction / *kyū-nobi* 急伸び rapid rise, steep rise, rapid growth / *En wa 1 doru=131en-dai zenpan e kyū-nobi* 円は1ドル=131円台前半へ急伸び The yen rapidly increased against the dollar to the lower reaches of 131 / *kyū-seichō* 急成長 rapid growth

kyūnobi 急伸 rapid growth, rapid increase

*kyūshin 急伸 misreading for *kyūnobi*

kyūshū 吸収 absorption
shikin o kyūshū suru 資金を吸収する absorb capital / *Nichigin wa kijitsu o mukaeta kai-ope tegata 4,000-oku-en no uchi 2,000-oku-en o kessai shite shikin o kyūshū* 日銀は期日を迎えた買いオペ手形4000億円のうち

2000億円を決済して資金を吸収 The Bank of Japan approved the absorption of ¥200 billion of ¥400 billion in buying operation bills which had reached maturity / *kyūshū gappei* 吸収合併 take-over / *kyūshū gōben* 吸収合弁 merger

kyū-Soren 旧ソ連 former Soviet Union

kyūtō 急騰 boost, sharp rise, spurt

kyūzō 急増 rapid increase, rapid growth, sudden increase

M

machimachi まちまち mixed
machimachi no sōba tenkai datta まちまちの相場展開だった Trading was generally mixed

mado 窓 window
madoguchi 窓口 window (into a concern, or the main contact point with a company or organization), counter, over-the counter (see also *tentō* 店頭) / *madoguchi hanbai* 窓口販売 'over-the counter' sales / *madoguchi sōba* 窓口 相場 over-the counter rates / *madohan* 窓販 (*madoguchi hanbai* 窓口販売) 'over the counter' sales

mājā マージャー merger
also *baishū* 買収

manki 満期 maturity
mankijitsu 満期日 due date, date of maturity / *manki ni tassuru* 満期に達す る mature

manshion マンション condominium
The word マンション is presumably, and rather incongruously, borrowed from the English 'mansion' i.e a very large, imposing house

maruyū マル優 non-tax system for small savings

tokubetsu maruyū 特別マル優 small amount public bond interest exemption

masatsu 摩擦 friction
bōeki masatsu 貿易摩擦 trade friction / *masatsu kanwa* 摩擦緩和 relaxation of friction

mason 磨損 wear and tear
lit. 'friction' 磨 and 'loss' 損

mawari 回り return

medo メド prospect, outlook
saisan no medo ga tatanai/tsukanai 採算のメドが立たない/付かない prove unprofitable

meigara 名柄 brand, issue, stock, title of a security
ninki o yobu meigara 人気を呼ぶ 名柄 'hot issue' (lit. 'stock' 名柄 which 'invites' 呼ぶ 'popularity' 人気) / *aru meigara o torihikijo de baibai suru koto no kyoka* ある名柄を取引所で販売することの許可 The admission of a security to be traded on the stock exchange / *yūryō meigara* 優良名柄 prime issue / *meigara-sū* 名柄数 (number of) issues

meigi 名義 name, title
meigi kakikae 名義書換 transfer of a name or title / *meigi kakigae daikō kikan* 名義書換代行機関 transfer agent / *meigi kashi* 名義貸し 'lending street names' / *meigi nin* 名義人 nominee

meimoku 名目 nominal
meimoku gakumen 名目額面 nominal par / *meimoku gakumen kabushiki* 名目額面株式 nominal par value stock

memori 目盛り scale, gradation
Lines on a graph are often labelled *hidari-memori* 左目盛り and *migi-memori* 右目盛り indicating which scale, left or right, the line refers to

menjo 免除 exemption
tōroku menjo torihikisho (also *tōroku menjo torihikijo*) 登録免除取引所 exempt stock exchange / *menjo shōken* 免除証券 exempt security

mi- 未 'not yet'

mi-hakkō kabushiki 未発行株式 unissued stock (lit. 'not yet' 未 'issued' 発行 'stock' 株式) / *mi-shiharai haito* 未支払い配当 unpaid dividends, arrearage

mikomi 見込み prospects
  that is, for the present fiscal year, as opposed to *jisseki* 実績, the actual results for the last and previous years, and *yosoku* 予測, the predictions or forecasts for the next and subsequent fiscal years / *tōsho mikomi* 当初見込み initial prospect

mikoshi 見越し anticipation
  sakidaka mikoshi 先高見越し anticipation of a rise

mikosu 見越すanticipate
  Juyōsha ga neagari o mikoshite zaiko-gai ni hashitta 需要者が値上がりを見越して在庫買いに走ったThe demand sector anticipated price rises and rushed to build up stocks

mikuro keizai ミクロ経済 microeconomics

miokuru 見送る mark time, wait and see
  lit. 'see off', 'see' 見 and 'send' 送る

miryokuteki 魅力的 attractive
  miryokuteki na shūeki 魅力的な収益 attractive profit

mizumashi kabu 水増し株 watered stock
  lit. 'water' 水 'added' 増し 'stock' 株 (see also *mizuwari kabu* 水割り株) / *mizuwari kabu* 水割り株 watered-down, diluted stock (lit. 'water' 水 'diluting' 割り, from *waru* 割る 'dilute' or 'split' and 'stock' 株) 水割り by itself means a Scotch with water

mochikabu 持株 equity share, shareholdings
  mochikabu kaisha (also *mochikabu gaisha*) 持株会社 holding company (lit. 'company' 会社 which 'holds' (*motsu*) 持 the 'stock' 株) / see also *oya kaisha* 親会社

mokuhyō 目標 target

mokuromi-sho 目論見書 a prospectus
  lit. 'plan' 目論見 'document' 書

63

monitaringu モニタリング monitoring
also *kanshi* 監視

-mono もの lot, delivery
Torihiki no chūshin de aru 9-gatsu-mono wa 1-bareru=20.05 -10 to zenjitsu owari-ne hi 0.025-doru-daka to natte iru 取引の中心である９月ものは１バレル = 20.05-10と前日 終り値比0.025ドル高となっている The key September delivery stood at 20.05-10 dollars per barrel, up 0.025 from the previous day's close

motochō 元帳 ledger

moyō nagame 模様眺め players on the sidelines, wait-and-see
Ō bike ni kake moyō nagame kibun ga tsuyomatta 大引けに掛け模様眺め気分が強まった Stock prices closed slightly lower (lit. 'At close of trading the wait-and-see mood strengthened')

mu-gakumen 無額面 non-par
mu-gakumen kabu 無額面株 non-par stock / *mu-gakumen kabushiki* 無額面株式 non-par stock

mugen 無限 unlimited
mugen sekinin shain 無限責任社員 general partner (lit. 'unlimited' 無限、'responsibility' 責任 'company member' 社員)

mujin 無尽 inexhaustible
mujin kaisha (also *mujin gaisha*) 無尽会社 mutual financing association, mutual loan company

mu-jōken 無条件 unconditional
kōru mu-jōken-mono コール無条件もの unconditional call loan / *kōru mu-jōken-mono rēto* コール無条件ものレート rate for unconditional call loan / *mu-jōken-mono* 無条件もの unconditional call loan, unconditionals

mukei 無形 intangible
mukei shisan 無形資産 intangible assets (c.f. *yūkei shisan* 有形資産 tangible assets)

mu-kigen 無期限 open, unlimited
mu-kigen chūmon 無期限注文 open order

mu-kimei 無記名 blank, uninscribed, unregistered
mu-kimei sai 無記名債 bearer bond

mushō 無償 without compensation, without cost, gratuitous
mushō kōfu 無償交付 free distribution

mu-tanpo 無担保 unsecured, without collateral
mutanpo kashitsuke 無担保貸付け straight loan / *mutanpo kashitsuke kin* 無担保貸付け金 unsecured loan / *mutanpo saiken* 無担保債券 debenture, plain bond

N

naibu 内部 inside
kaisha naibu 会社内部 inside a company / *kaisha naibu no jōhō* 会社内部の情報 inside information

naigai 内外 domestic and overseas
naigai kakakusa kaishō 内外価格差解消 removal of differentials between prices in Japan and overseas

naiju 内需 domestic demand
kokunai juyō 国内需要 / *naiju kakudai* 内需拡大 expansion in domestic demand

nakadachi 仲立ち broker, middleman

nami 並 ordinary
nami-gawase 並為替 ordinary remittance

nanchō 軟調 easing, softening

nariyuki 成り行き course of events
nariyuki chūmon 成り行き注文 carte blanch order, order without limit, market order (lit. 'order' *chūmon* 注文 which is left to the 'course of events' 成り行き)

nashikuzushi 済し崩し phasing out, sapping

also: pay back in instalments, amortize / *Hinshitsu kōjō no kosuto-daka wa nashikuzushi ni sareta* 品質向上のコスト高は済し崩しにされた The high costs of quality improvement were amortized

Nazudakku ナズダック NASDAQ
National Association of Securities Dealers Automated Quotation

ne 値 price
neagari 値上がり price-rise / *nedan* 値段 price / *ōbike nedan* 大引け値段 closing price, closing quotation, finish / *negoro* 値ごろ suitable price / *negoro-gai* 値ごろ買い bargain-hunting / *negoro-kan* 値ごろ感 bargain hunting / *Negoro-kan kara no kai mo haitte ori, FT-hyakushu wa zenmen-daka de suii shite iru* 値ごろ感からの買いも入っており、FT百種は全面高で推移している Stock prices rose across the board on bargain-hunting

nekizami 値刻み (in) variations
Yobine wa 8-bun-no-1 doru no nekizami de tonaerareru 呼び値は8分の1ドル値刻みで唱えられる Bids and offers are made in variations of 1/8 of $1 per share

nendo 年度 fiscal year
in contrast to *rekinen* 歴年 'calendar year' / see also *kaikei nendo* 会計年度 / *ka-nendo* 過年度 preceding financial year

nenkin 年金 annuity, pension, pension plan
nenkin shintaku 年金信託 pension trusts

neugoki 値動き price changes, price movements, gains or losses

nezaya 値ザヤ spread, margin
nezaya kasegi 値ザヤ稼ぎ profit-taking arbitrage transactions

nibui 鈍い inert, slow-witted, thick-headed (of investors)

Nichigin 日銀 Bank of Japan (BoJ)
(*Nihon (Nippon) Ginkō* 日本銀行) / *Nichigin-ken* 日銀券 Bank of Japan bonds / *Nichigin ope-bun* 日銀オペ分 proportion of bills operated by the Bank of Japan

nigawase 荷為替 documentary bill (draft)

nigawase tegata 荷為替手形 exchange bill

Nikkei Heikin 日経平均 Nikkei Stock Average

Nikkei Heikin wa koguchi no indekkusu-uri nado ni osarete kyūsoku ni nobinayami, koyasuku hiketa 日経平均は小口のインデックス売りなどに押されて急速に伸び悩み、小安く引けた The Nikkei Stock Average, forced down by small-lot index selling and so on, rapidly slackened, and finished weak / *Nikkei Heikin Kabuka* 日経平均株価 Nikkei Stock Average / *Nikkei 300* 日経平均株価 300 Nikkei 300 weighted stock price average

ninki 人気 popularity, mood, market sentiment

kanetsu ninki no shinkabu 過熱人気の新株 an overheated new issue / *ninki o yobu meigara* 人気を呼ぶ銘柄 a hot issue (lit. an 'issue' 銘柄 which 'attracts' 呼ぶ 'popularity' 人気) / *ninki kabu* 人気株 active stock, star performer

ninshō 認証 certification (i.e. of imports)

kijun, ninshō tetsuzuki no kaizen 基準、認証手続きの改善 improvement in standards and certification procedures

*nippo 日歩 misreading for *hibu*

nishigawa 西側 the West

nobinayamu 伸び悩む to slow down, level off, be stagnant

nokinami ni 軒並みに across the board

lit. from 'house' to house 軒 'alike' 並 / ...*Nihon, Amerika, Berugii nado shuyōkoku ga nokinami ni zōsan to natta* ...日本、アメリカ、ベルギーなど主要国が軒並みに増産となった...leading countries such as Japan, the US and Belgium increased production across the board

nomi-koi 飲みこい bucketing

nomi-koi sōba-shi 飲みこい相場師 bucket-shop operator, bucketeer / *nomi-ya* 飲み屋 bucket-shop operator, outside broker

norikae 乗り換え switching

nōryoku 能力 capacity

seizō nōryoku 製造能力 production capacity

noseru 乗せる reach
see ...*dai ni noseru* 台に乗せる

nōzei 納税 payment of taxes
nōzei junbi yokin 納税準備預金 deposit for tax payments / *nōzeisha* 納税者 taxpayer / *tagaku nōzeisha* 多額納税者 upper-bracket taxpayer

nyūsatsu 入札 bidding
...*kakaku de nyūsatsu suru* 価格で入札する bid at such -and -such a price / *kyōsō nyūsatsu* 競争入札 competitive bidding / *nyūsatsu kakaku* 入札価格 bid price

O

ōbike 大引け the close of the market
ōbike nedan 大引け値段 closing quotation, finish / *ōbike ni kake(te)* 大引けに掛け(て) at close of business

ōbo 応募 subscription
ōbo-sū 応募数 number of subscriptions, rate of subscription

ochiiru 陥る to fall into
keiei kiken ni ochiiru 経営危険に陥る have a management crisis

ōdai 大台 barrier
ōdai-kawari (also *ōdai-gawari*) 大台変わり reaching the barrier (same as *ōdai-nose* 大台乗せ) / *ōdai-nose* 大台乗せ reaching the barrier (of e.g. ¥200, with regard to a price previously of ¥199 or below) / *ōdai-ware* 大台割れ falling below the barrier (of e.g.¥200, with regard to a price previously of ¥201 or above)

odoriba 踊り場 landing (in or at the top of a flight of stairs)
also: resting place / *89-nen wa kanetsu kara antei e mukau odoriba to natta to ieru* 89年は過熱から安定に向かう踊り場になったと言える 1989 marked the transition from a period of overheating to a period of stability

ōgata 大型 large-scale
ōgata kabu 大型株 large-capital stock (such as *tekkō kabu* 鉄鋼株 steel

stock, and *zōsen kabu* 造船株 shipbuilding stock, etc.) / *tekkō , zōsen nado ōgata kabu ga kenchō de...* 鉄鋼、造船など大型株が堅調で... steel, shipbuilding and other large-capital stock were firm... / *Zenba wa kōteki shisan, tōshi shintaku ga ōgata kabu ni kai o ire shikkari shita tenkai datta ga...* 前場は公的資産、投資信託が大型株に買いを入れしっかりした展開だったが... The morning session showed a hiccup in buying large-capital stock by public assets and investment trusts, but... / *ōgata koruri tenpo* 大型小売り店舗 large retail store

ōhaba 大幅 large-scale
ōhaba geraku 大幅下落 steep fall

oiru オイル oil
oiru darā sai オイル・ダラー債 oil-dollar denominated bond / *oiru shokku* オイル・ショック oil crisis

oishō 追い証 remargin, more margin

oiuchi 追い撃ち pursue, follow, rout an enemy
oiuchi o kakete 追い撃ちを掛けて in close pursuit of, following up behind

oiyaru 追い遣る chase away, drive out, order out
Naganen ni wataru sekai-teki na fero shirikon fukyō wa, Nihon nomi narazu sekai-jū no fero shirikon mēkā o kyushi, heisa, tettai e to oiyatta 長年にわたる世界的なフェロ・シリコン不況は、日本のみならず世界中のフェロ・シリコン・メーカーを休止、閉鎖、撤退へと追い遣った The worldwide slump in ferro silicon, which has continued for many years, has driven ferro silicon manufacturers, not only in Japan but all over the world, to stoppages, closures and withdrawals from the industry

ōkabunushi 大株主 big shareholder, big stockholder

oku 億 100m
In order to convert *oku* 億 to billions, i.e. thousand-millions, move the decimal point one digit to the left: thus, *2,100.00-oku* = 210.00 billion / *nisen-hyakuoku-en* 二千百億円 ¥210 bn

omoshiromi ga nai 面白みがない stodgy

omowaku 思惑 expectation, speculation

Basically, 'thinking of something', 'having something on one's mind'. Thus, *omowaku onna* 思惑女 'a woman one is fond of'. But in the financial field, 思惑 gives rise to *omowaku-chigai* 思惑違い 'misjudgement in speculation' *omowaku-shi* 思惑師 'speculator', and *omowaku-suji* 思惑筋 'speculative interests' / *Bei-bōeki akaji kakudai e no omowaku* 米貿易赤字拡大への思惑 The expectation of an increased US trade deficit / *omowaku-chigai* 思惑違い misjudgement in speculation / *omowaku-shi* 思惑師 speculator / *omowaku-suji* 思惑筋 speculative interests

ope オペ operation
short for *operēshon* オペレーション) / *ope-bun* オペ分 proportion of bills etc operated by / *Nichigin ope-bun* 日銀オペ分 proportion of bills operated by the Bank of Japan

ōpun オープン open, open-ended
ōpun kinri オープン金利 open rates / *ōpun kinri to tegata rēto no kakusa ga shukushō shite kita* オープン金利と手形レートの格差が縮小して来た The differential between open rates and bill rates has narrowed

opushion オプション option call
opushion kōshi オプション行使 the implementation of an option call

ōrai sōba 往来相場 rise-and-fall market

Ō shu 欧州 Europe
Ō shu tsuka shijō 欧州通貨市場 European currency market(s), Euro-dollar market / *Ō shu Yotaku Shōken* 欧州預託証券 European Depositary Receipts (EDR)

ōte 大手 large
ōte shōken kaisha (also *ōte shōken gaisha*) 大手証券会社 first-tier securities house / *jun-ōte shoken kaisha* 準大手証券会社 second-tier securities house

oya-kaisha 親会社 parent company, holding company
also *oya-gaisha* / see also *mochikabu gaisha* 持ち株会社

ōzoko 大底 major bottom

P

peseta ペセタ peseta
Supein 100 peseta スペイン100ペセタ 100 Spanish pesetas

pondo ポンド pound
Ei-pondo 英ポンド UK sterling

pōtoforio ポートフォリオ portfolio
pōtoforio tōshi ポートフォリオ投資 portfolio management, investment
management

puraimu rēto プライム・レート prime rate, prime interest rate

puranto プラント plant, installation

pūru-sei kumiai sōsa プール制組合操作 pool operation

putto-opushion プット・オプション put option

R

rekinen 暦年 calendar year
as opposed to *(kaikei) nendo* 会計年度 'fiscal year'

renketsu 連結 consolidated, connection, coupling
renketsu gyōseki 連結業績 consolidated results / *renketsu zaimu shohyō* 連
結財務諸表 consolidated statement

Renpō Junbi Seido 連邦準備制度 Federal Reserve System
of the US

renzoku 連続 continual, consecutive, serial
gogatsu-matsu ikō sankagetsu renzoku no zandaka genshō 五月末以降
三ヶ月連続の残高減少 third consecutive monthly fall since May / *renzoku*

shōkan hōshiki 連続償還方式 serial repayment method / *renzoku shōkan saiken* 連続償還債券 serial bond

rēto レート a rate

kōru mujōken rēto コール無条件レート unconditional call loan / *tegata rēto* 手形レート bill rate

rieki 利益 profit, earnings

rieki o umu 利益を産む make a profit / *eigyō rieki* 営業利益 operating profits / *hitokabu-atari no rieki* 一株当たりの利益 earnings per share /*keijō rieki* 経常利益 recurring profit, pre-tax profit / *rinji rieki* 臨時利益 non-recurrent earnings / *ryūho rieki* 留保利益 retained earnings, reinvested earnings, earned surplus / *zeibiki rieki* 税引き利益 after-tax earnings / *rieki jōyo kin* 利益剰余金 earned surplus / *rieki sanka shasai* 利益参加社債 participating bond

rifuda 利札 coupon

see *risatsu* 利札

rigui 利喰い profit-taking, profit-cashing, realization

Zenjitsu no ōhaba jōshō ni taishite rigui no uri ga yaya dete iru 前日の大幅上昇に対して利食いの売りがやや出ている Traders took profits after the previous day's sharp rise

riisu リース lease

riisu bukken リース物件 leased properties / *riisu bukken chinshaku ryō* リース物件賃借料 rent for leased properties

rikin 利金 interest-earning funds

*rikkai 立会 misreading for *tachiai*

rikō 履行 fulfil

furikō 不履行 non-fulfilment / *saimu furikō* 債務不履行 inability to repay debts

rimawari 利回り returns, yield

lit. 'profit' 利 coming full 'circle'回り / *kabushiki rimawari* 株式利回り dividend yield / *kikan-betsu rimawari* 期間別利回り yield curve (lit. 'yield' 利回り 'by' 別 'term' 期間) / *kō-rimawari* 高利回り high rate of income, good yield / *saishū rimawari* 最終利回り yield to maturity / *rimawari hyō* 利回り表 yield book

rinji 臨時 special, non-recurrent, incidental, extra
rinji rieki 臨時利益 non-recurrent earnings / *rinji son'eki kōmoku* 臨時損益項目 non-recurrent item / *rinji sonshitsu* 臨時損失 non-recurrent deduction

riritsu 利率 interest rate

risaikuru リサイクル recycling
shigen risaikuru 資源リサイクル the recycling of resources

risatsu (also **rifuda**) **利札** coupon
risatsu no nai saimu 利札のない債務 non-interest bearing obligations

*risaya 利鞘 misreading for *rizaya*

rishi 利子 interest
rishi o shiharau 利子を支払う pay interest / *keika rishi* 経過利子 accrued interest

*rishō 利鞘 misreading for *rizaya*

rishoku 利殖 making money

*rishoku 利喰 misreading for *rigui* 利喰い

risutora リストラ restructuring
short for *risutorakucharingu* リストラクチャリング

riten 利点 advantage
riten o kyōju suru 利点を享受する obtain advantages

ritsu 率 rate
kabuka shūeki ritsu 株価収益率 price earning ratio (PER) / *waribiki ritsu* 割引率 discount rate / *ritsuki* 利付き with profit / *ritsuki kin'yū sai* 利付き金融債 coupon bank debenture, interest-bearing bank debenture / *ritsuki sai* 利付債 coupon bond / *ritsuki shōken* 利付き証券 with-interest security / *kakutei ritsuki shōken* 確定利付き証券 fixed-interest security / *ritsuki shōsho* 利付証書 interest-bearing certificate

riyōsha 利用車 (passenger) automobile

rizaya 利鞘 interest margin, spread

rōbai 狼狽 confusion, panic, dismay
rōbai uri 狼狽売り blind sale

rōreika 老齢化 ageing
rōreika shakai 老齢化社会 the ageing society (in which the welfare of the elderly has an increasing effect on personal and public finances)

ruiseki 累積 cumulative
ruiseki tōhyō ken 累積投票権 cumulative voting / *ruiseki sonshitsu* 累積損失 cumulative loss / *ruiseki yūsen kabu* 累積優先株 cumulative preferred stock

rūru ルール rules
Kyoninka ya kisei nado, doko made seifu ga kan'yo suru no ka no rūru o hakkiri sase, takoku-kan de chōsei shite takoku no shisutemu o chōwa sasete iku 許認可や規制など、どこまで政府が関与するのかのルールをはっきりさせ、多国間で調整して多国のシステムを調和させて行く To clarify the rules as to how far Government will take part in certification and regulation, and to harmonize various countries' systems through international cooperation

ryō 量 volume
e.g. volume of imports as opposed to value *gaku* 額

ryōdate 両建て option, compensating deposit
Must retain a part of the amount lent at the time of lending. See also *buzumi* 歩積み / *ryōdate yōkin* 両建て預金 compensating balance

ryōga 凌駕 excel, surpass, outdo
Kabuka ga heikin kakaku o chōkikan ni watatte ryōga suru 株価が平均価格を長期間にわたって凌駕する The share price, over the long term, exceeds the average price

*ryōken 両建 misreading for *ryōdate* 両建て

ryōshūshō 領収証 or *ryōshūsho* 領収書 receipt

*ryōtate 両建 misreading for *ryōdate* 両建て

ryūdō 流動 current, floating, liquid
ryūdō fusai 流動負債 current liabilities / *ryūdō shisan* 流動資産 current assets, floating assets, liquid floating assets / *shūmi ryūdō shisan* 正味流動資産 net current assets, working capital / *ryūdōsei yochokin* 流動性預貯金 instant-access deposits and savings accounts

ryūho 留保 retain
ryūho rieki 留保利益 retained earnings, earned surplus, reinvested earnings

ryūtsū 流通 distribution
ryūtsū kabu 流通株 distribution industry stock / *ryūtsū shijō* 流通市場 secondary market (as opposed to *hakkō shijō* 発行市場 primary market), distribution sector / *ryūtsū shōken* 流通証券 negotiable instrument

S

sabaku 裁く handle, decide
chūmon o sabaku 注文を裁く handle an order

sābisu サービス services (as a category of equities)

saeki 差益 marginal profits
shōkan saeki bun 償還差益分 accretion, accumulation

sagaku 差額 mark-up, differential
sagaku no nashikuzushi-bun 差額の済し崩し分 amortization

sai 債 bond
usually found in combination, as in *saiken* 債券 'bond' / *Ajia doru-sai* アジア・ドル債 Asian-dollar bond / *genbutsu-sai* 現物債 cash bond / *karikae-sai* 借換え債 refunding bond, roll-over bond / *kimei-sai* 記名債 registered bond / *kōri-sai* 高利債 high interest bond / *kōsha-sai* 公社債 bonds, bonds and debentures / *Kōsha-Sai Hikiuke Kyōkai* 社債引受協会 Bond Underwriters Association / *mukimei-sai* 無記名債 bearer bond / *NTT-sai* NTT

債 NTT (Nippon Telegraph and Telephone Corporation) bonds / *ritsuki kin'yū-sai* 利付金融債 coupon bank debenture, interest-bearing bank debenture / *ritsuki-sai* 利付債 coupon bond / *seifu hoshō-sai* 政府保証債 government-guaranteed bond / *teiri-sai* 低利債 low interest bond / *waribiki kinyū-sai* 割引金融債 discount bank debenture

saiken 債券 bond, debenture security

kōgai bōshi shisetsu muke saiken 公害防止施設向け債券 pollution control bond / *kōteki jūtaku kensetsu shikin muke saiken* 公的住宅建設資金向け債券 public housing agency bond / *mu-tanpo saiken* 無担保債券 debenture bond, plain bond / *renzoku shōkan saiken* 連続償還債券 serial bond / *sangyō yūchi muke saiken* 産業誘致向け債券 industrial revenue bonds / *shinkabu hikiukeken-tsuki saiken* 新株引受権付き債券 bond with subscription right, bond with pre-emptive right / *shōken tanpo-tsuki saiken* 証券担保付き債券 collateral trust bond / *tanpo-tsuki saiken* 担保付き債券 mortgage bond / *saiken hakkōsha* 債券発行者 bond issuer / *saiken sakimono* 債券先物 bond futures / *saiken shoyūsha* 債券所有者 bond-holder

saikensha 債券者 creditor

Chōtanki no saikensha yori kashitsukerareta shihon 長短期の債権者より貸し付けられた資本 Capital financed by long- and short-term creditors

saiken 再建 rebuilding, reorganization

saimu 債務 debt, liabilities

risatsu no nai saimu 利札のない債務 non-interest bearing obligations / *saimu furikō* 債務不履行 inability to meet obligations / *saimusha* 債務者 (also *saimu shoyūsha* 債務所有者) debtor / *saimu waribiki shōkyaku* 債務割引償却 amortization of discount on funded debt

saisan 採算 profitability

saisan no medo ga tatanai / tsukanai 採算のメドが立たない / 付かない to prove unprofitable / *saisan sure-sure* 採算すれすれ barely profitable (すれすれ means 'having a close shave', 'just skim the surface of the water')

saishō hendō bun 最小変動分 minimum fractional change

sai-shutoku 再取得 repurchase

saishū rimawari 最終利回り yield to maturity

saitei 裁定 arbitrate

Kai ichijun-go wa saitei kaishō ni tomonau genbutsu kabu-uri ni osareta 買い一巡後は裁定解消に伴う現物株売りにおされた After brief buying, market players were forced to sell spot shares while cancelling arbitrage

saitori 才取り jobber, specialist

sakanoboru 遡る trace back to, back-date, be retrospective to

Yakuin hōshū no shōkaku o kongetsu shigatsu ni sakanobotte tōketsu suru 役員報酬の昇格を今月4月に遡って凍結する A freeze in rises in executives' remunerations, retroactive to this past April

saki 先 destination

torihiki-saki 取引先 client / *kariire-saki* 借入れ先 channel for raising funds / *sakidaka* 先高 future rise, advance, higher quotations for future months / *sakidaka-kan* 先高感 anticipation of a rise / *Beikoku de kinri no sakidaka-kan ga tsuyomatte iru* 米国で金利の先高感が強まっている There is heightened anticipation of a rise in interest rates in the United States / *sakidaka mikoshi* 先高見越し anticipation of an advance, anticipation of a rise

sakimono 先物 futures

saiken sakimono 債券先物 bond futures / *Sakimono sōba no yoritsuki o matte yōsumi-kibun ga tsuyoi* 先物相場の寄り付きを待って様子見気分が強い Players stayed on the sidelines awaiting opening developments in the futures market

sakugen 削減 reduction

-san 産 product of

Chūgoku-san 中国産 Chinese product

sangyō 産業 industry

Eikoku Sangyō Renmei 英国産業連盟 Confederation of British Industry (CBI) / *sangyō yūchi (muke) saiken* 産業誘致 (向け) 債券 industrial revenue bonds (lit. 'bonds' 債券 'directed towards' 向け the 'attraction' 誘致 of ' industry' 産業)

sanka 参加 participation

rieki sanka shasai 利益参加社債 participating bond / *sanka-teki yūsen kabushiki* 参加的優先株式 participation preferred stock (c.f. *hi-sanka-teki yūsen kabushiki* 非参加的優先株式 'non-participatory preferred stock')

sannyū 参入 participate, join, be a player in a market
Beikoku wa Nihon shijō ni sannyū dekinai haigō ni Nihon no keizai shakai shisutemu sono mono ga aru koto ni kizuita 米国は日本市場に参入出来ない背後に、日本の経済社会システムそのものがある事に気がついた The US noticed that behind the fact that it cannot be a player in the Japanese market lies Japan's very economic and social system

sanpatsu 散発 sporadic
sanpatsu yasu 散発安 sporadic fall / *Seimitsu, kagaku, kin'yū kabu mo sanpatsu yasu* 精密、化学、金融株も散発安 Precision instruments, chemical products and financial stock fell sporadically

sanshutsu 産出 output

sashine 指し値 bid, bid price, limit
gyaku-sashine 逆指し値 counter-bid / *gyaku-sashine chūmon* 逆指し値注文 stop-order, stop-loss order / *sashine chūmon* 指し値注文 limited (stop) order, straddled order

sason 差損 difference, differential
kawase sason 為替差損 losses arising from the difference in currency quotations

saya 鞘 spread, margin, brokerage
rizaya 利鞘 profit margin of interest rate, interest rate spread / *sayatori* 鞘取り arbitrage, profit-taking

sayō 作用 action, work, operation, effect
Kaisha wa teko no sayō o okiku riyō shite iru 会社はテコの作用を大きく利用している The company is highly geared / *teko sayō* テコ作用 leverage

sayū 左右 control
lit. 'left and right' / *Sōba o sayū suru shinki zairyō ga naku, neugoki wa chiisai* 相場を左右する新規材料がなく、値動きは小さい Prices moved within a narrow range, reflecting the lack of fresh incentives in the market

Segin 世銀 World Bank
short for *Sekai Ginkō* 世界銀行

seichō 成長 growth
> *kyū-seichō* 急成長 rapid growth / *seichō kabu* 成長株 growth stock / *seichō ritsu* 成長率 growth rate

seido 制度 system
> *kijun ninshō seido* 基準認証制度 system of standards and certification / *Renpō Junbi Seido* 連邦準備制度 Federal Reserve System (of the US) / *ukewatashi seido* 受け渡し制度 five-day delivery plan

seifu 政府 government
> *seifu hakkō yūka shōken* 政府発行有価証券 gilt-edged security / *seifu hoshō sai* 政府保証債 government-guaranteed bond, contingency debt / *seifu tanki shōken* 政府短期証券 short-term government securities, government bills

seigen 制限 restrictions
> *kinkyū yunyū seigen* 緊急輸入制限 safeguards (lit. 'emergency' 緊急 'importers' 輸入 'limits' 制限)

*seigin 世銀 misreading for *segin*

seiho 生保 life assurance
> short for *seimei hoken* 生命保険

*seimi 正味 misreading for *shōmi*

seimitsu 精密 precision, precision machinery and tools
> *yusō seimitsu* 輸送精密 transport and precision tools (as a category of equities) / *seimitsu kabu* 精密株 (short for *seimitsu kikai kabu* 精密機械株) precision instruments stock

seiri 整理 liquidation, winding-up
> *kaisha seiri* 会社整理 termination of a business (by the conversion of its assets into cash) / *zaiko seiri* 在庫整理 inventories adjustment / *zaiko seiri ga susumi, shinausukan ga shijō shinri o aorihajimeta* 在庫整理 が進み、品薄感が市場心理を煽り始めた Inventories adjustment continued, and scarcities began to add fuel to the market's fears

seiritsu-bi 成立日 date of transaction
> see *baibai seiritsu-bi* 売買成立日

seisaku 政策 policy

kyōtsū tsūshō seisaku 共通通商政策 common trade policy / *tai-Nichi tsūshō seisaku* 対日通商政策 trade policies with regard to Japan / *tsūsan seisaku* 通産政策 policies on trade and industry / *tsūshō seisaku* 通商政策 trade policy

seisan 清算 clearing

seisanji 清算時 time of settlement / *seisan kachi* 清算価値 break-up value, liquidation

seizō 製造 production

seizō nōryoku 製造能力 production capacity

Sekai Ginkō 世界銀行 World Bank

also *Segin* 世銀

seki 関 see *seki-no-yama* 関の山

sekinin 責任 responsibility

mugen sekinin shain 無限責任社員 general partner

seki-no-yama 関の山 a loser's game, the best one can do

also: the utmost one can expect / *Shakkin o sezu ni iru no ga seki-no-yama da* 借金をせずにいるのが関の山だ It is all I can do to keep out of debt / The 関 or 関所 was a checking station between provinces in pre-modern Japan. Movement by the population was controlled. If one wanted to disown debts or other difficulties, one fled with false papers to the nearest 'checking station' 関 in the 'mountains' 山 in order to escape to a neighbouring province

sekiyu 石油 petroleum

kagaku sekiyu 化学石油 chemical & petroleum (as a category of equities) / *sekiyu kiki* 石油危機 oil crisis / *sekiyu shokku* 石油ショック crisis

sen 千 1,000

2,100-oku-en 2100億円 ¥210bn / *Gozen 9-ji genzai 1-doru=127-en 15-25-sen to zenjitsu owarine-hi 10-sen no en-daka-doru-yasu to natte iru* 午前9時現在 1 ドル = 127円15-25銭と前日終わり値比10銭の円高ドル安となっている As of 9 am the dollar opened somewhat lower than Tokyo's closing price to stand at 127.15-25 yen, down 0.10 from the previous day's close

sen'i 繊維 textiles fibres
sen'i kami 繊維紙 textiles & paper (as a category of equities)

senmu 専務 executive director
also *senmu torishimariyaku* / see also *shachō* 社長 president / *fuku-shachō* 副社長 vice-president / *kaichō* 会長 chairman / *jōmu* 常務 (also *jōmu torishimariyaku*) managing director / *buchō* 部長 divisional director / *kachō* 課長 sectional head / *senmu torishimariyaku* 専務取締役 (also *senmu* 専務) executive director

senshinkoku 先進国 leading nation
senshikoku shunō kaigi 先進国首脳会議 Summit meeting of the Group of Seven industrialized nations

seri 競り auction
see also *kyōsō* 競争) / *seri baibai* 競り売買 auction, buying and selling by auction (see also *kyōsō baibai* 競争売買)

setsubi 設備 plant and equipment, installations
setsubi shintaku shōsho 設備信託証書 equipment trust certificates / *setsubi tōshi* 設備投資 capital investment (in plant and equipment)

settei 設定 set up
teitōken setteisha 抵当権設定者 mortgager

sewanin kai 世話人会 bond facilitation committee
in terms of long-term government bonds

shachō 社長 president
see also *fuku-shachō* 副社長 vice-president / *kaichō* 会長 chairman / *senmu* 専務 (also *senmu torishimariyaku* 専務取締役) executive director / *jōmu* 常務 (also *jōmu torishimariyaku* 常務取締役) managing director / *buchō* 部長 divisional director / *kachō* 課長 sectional head

shain 社員 company employee
mugen sekinin shain 無限責任社員 general partner

shakkuri しゃっくり hiccup
Zenba wa kōteki shisan, tōshi shintaku ga ōgata kabu ni kai o ire shikkari shita tenkai datta ga... 前場は公的資産、投資信託が大型株に買

いを入れしゃっかりした展開だったが... The morning session showed a hiccup in buying large-capital stock by public assets and investment trusts, but...

*shakunyū 借入 misreading for *kariire*

shasai 社債 bond or stock, industrial or corporate bond or debenture
futsū shasai 普通社債 straight bond / *kōsha sai* 公社債 public and corporate bonds, government bonds and corporate debentures / *rieki sanka shasai* 利益参加社債 participating bond / *shūeki shasai* 収益社債 income bonds, adjustment bond / *tenkan shasai* 転換社債 convertible bond, convertible debenture, mezzanine money

shibo 私募 private
shibo hakkō 私募発行 private placement

shidan 師団 syndicate
hikiuke shidan 引受師団 underwriting syndicate

shihai 支配 control
keiei-ken shihai 経営権支配 takeover

shiharai 支払い payment
shiharai funō 支払い不能 insolvency (lit. 'inability' 不能 to 'pay' 支払い) / *shiharai kinri* 支払い金利 interest on payments / *shiharau* 支払う pay / *rishi o shiharau* 利子を支払う pay interest

shihon 資本 capital, capital stock, stockholders' equity, funds
anzen shihon 安全資本 security capital / *chōki shihon* 長期資本 long-term capital / *chōki shihon torihiki shijō* 長期資本取引市場 capital market (c.f. *tanki kin'yū shijō* 短期金融市場 money market) / *jiko shihon* 自己資本 funds on hand, equities / *juken shihon* 授権資本 authorised capital / *kin'yū shihon* 金融資本 financial capital / *kin'yū shihon shijō no kaihō* 金融資本市場の開放 liberalization of financial capital markets / *zengaku shihon no kogaisha* 全額資本の子会社 wholly-owned subsidiary / *shihon junbi kin* 資本準備金 capital reserve ('capital' 資本 'preparation' 準備 'money' 金) / *shihon kanjō* 資本勘定 net worth, stockholders' equity / *shihon kankei* 資本関係 capital ties / *shihon-kin* 資本金 capital, capital stock, stock capitalization / *shihon kōsei* 資本構成 capital structure, capital composition / *shihon shijō* 資本市場 capital market / *kin'yū shijō no kaihō* 金融市場の開放 liberalization of financial capital markets / *shihon shūsei* 資本修正 recapitalization,

capital revision

shijō 市場 market

aozora shijō 青空市場 open-air market (lit. 'blue' 青 'sky' *sora* 空 'market' 市場) / *chōki shihon torihiki shijō* 長期資本取引市場 capital market (c.f. *tanki kin'yū shijō* 短期金融市場 money market) / *gaikoku kawase shijō* 外国為替市場 foreign exchange (forex) market / *gensaki shijō* 現先市場 bond repurchase market / *hakkō shijō* 発行市場 primary market / *ippan kokyaku torihiki shijō* 一般顧客取引市場 outside market, retail market / *jiyū kyōsō baibai shijō* 自由競争売買市場 free auction market / *kakki aru shijō* 活気ある市場 vigorous market / *kin'yū shihon shijō* 金融資本市場 capital financial markets / *kin'yū shihon shijō no kaihō* 金融資本市場の開放 opening up of the capital financial, markets / *koritsuteki shijō* 効率的市場 efficient market / *Ō shū tsūka shijō* 欧州通貨市場 European currency market(s), Eurodollar market / *ryū tsū shijō* 流通市場 secondary market, distribution sector / *supotto shijō* スポット市場 spot market / *tanki kin'yū shijō* 短期金融市場 money market / *tentō shijō* 店頭市場 over-the-counter (OTC) market / *tsūka shijō* 通貨市場 currency market / *shijōsei* 市場性 marketability, saleability / *shijō shinri* 市場心理 market sentiment / *Zaiko seiri ga susumi, shinausu-kan ga shijō shinri o aorihajimeta* 在庫整理が進み、品薄感が市場心理を煽り始めた Inventories were liquidated, and scarcities began to add fuel to the market's fears

shijō 史上 historical

shijō saikō 史上最高 record high / *Zenjitsu no Nyū Yōku sōba ga shijō saikō ne o kōshin shite hiketa no o kōkan shite...* 前日のニューヨーク相場が史上最高値を更新して引けたのを好感して... Bolstered by another record high on the New York market of the previous day...

shika 市価 current price, market price, quotation

shi-kigyō 私企業 private company, private issuer

lit. 'private' 私 'enterprise' 企業

shikin 資金 capital, funds, financial resources

shikin o kyūshū suru 資金を吸収する absorb capital / *gensai shikin* 減債資金 sinking funds / *gensai shikin saiken* 減債資金債券 sinking funds bond / *haraikomi shikin* 払い込み資金 paid-up capital, capital stock paid in / *yoyū shikin* 余裕資金 surplus funds, lee-way / *shikin chō tatsu* 資金調達 raising capital / *shikin jukyū* 資金需給 supply and demand of capital / *shikin junkan*

資金循環 money flow, flow of funds, flow of accounts / *shikin un'yō* 資金運用 money management / *Shikin Un'yō-bu* 資金運用部 Trust Fund Bureau (of the Ministry of Finance) / *shikin yojō* 資金余剰 surplus of funds / *Shikin yojō jiai datta ga, kōru mu-jōken-mono rēto wa zenshumatsu-hi kawarazu no 4.0 pasento (dashite) ni sueokareta* 資金余剰地合だったが、コール無条件ものレートは前週末比 変わらずの4.0%(出手)に据え置かれた There was a general excess of funds, but the rate for unconditional call loans was 4.0% selling, unchanged from the previous weekend, and deferred / *shikinguri* 資金操り fund management, liquidity position, solvency / *shikinguri ga tsukanai* 資金操りが付かない have a liquidity crisis / *shikinguri-hyō* 資金操り表 money flow statement

shikkari しっかり firm, steady
also *kenchō* 堅調

shikkō 執行 execution
chūmon no shikkō 注文の執行 execution of order / *yuigon shikkōsha* 遺言執行者 executor

shikyō gyōsha 市況業者 private issuer

shinausu 品薄 scarcity of goods, shortage of stock
shinausu ni naru 品薄になる run short, become scarce / *shinausu kabu* 品薄株 narrow-market share, narrow-market stock, narrow-market security / *sinausu-kan* 品薄感 feeling of scarcity / *Zaiko sairi ga susumi, shinausu-kan ga shijō shinri o aorihajimeta* 在庫整理が進み、品薄感が市場を煽り始めた Inventories were liquidated, and scarcities began to add to the market's fears / *shinausu shōken* 品薄証券 narrow market security

shingapōru シンガポール Singapore
Shingapōru-doru シンガポールドル Singaporean dollar

shingi 審議 deliberation

shingikai 審議会 council
Kinri Chōsei Shingikai 金利調整審議会 Interest Adjustment Council / *Shōken Torihiki Shingikai* 証券取引審議会 Securities Exchange Council

shinkabu 新株 new issue, new stock
kanetsu ninki no shinkabu 過熱人気の新株 hot issue / *shinkabu*

hikiukeken-tsuki saiken 新株引受権付き債券 bond with pre-emptive right, bond with subscription right / *shinkabu hikiukeken-tsuki shasai* 新株引受権付き社債 corporate debenture with stock right / *shinkabu yūsen hikiuke-ken* 新株優先引受権 privileged subscription right

shinki 新規 new

kanetsu shinki no shinkabu 過熱新規の新株 overheated new issue / *shinki hakkō* 新規発行 new offering / *shinki zairyō* 新規材料 fresh incentives / *shinki zairyō-busoku* 新規材料不足 lack of fresh incentives / *Shinki zairyō-busoku de, akinai-usu no naka, shijō wa yōsumi kibun ga tsuyoi* 新規材料不足で、商い薄の中、市場は様子見気分が強い Players kept to the sidelines in thin trading due to a lack of fresh incentives / *shinki zairyō ni toboshii* 新規材料に乏しい lacking in fresh incentives

shinkin 信金 credit cooperative, credit union

shinpan 信販 selling credit, provision of credit

short for *shin'yō hanbai* 信用販売 / This has been the traditional source of credit for poorer people in Japan / *shinpan-gyō* 信販業 (traditional) credit-providing industry / *shinpan kādo* 信販カード plastic cards issued by *shinpan* 信販 credit sales companies

shinri 心理 psychology

shijō shinri 市場心理 market sentiment / *Zaiko sairi ga susumi, shinausu-kan ga shijō shinri o aorihajimeta* 在庫整理が進み、品薄感が市場を煽り始めた Inventories were liquidated, and scarcities began to add to the market's fears

shinsa 審査 credit analysis

shinseisho 申請書 application

jōjō shinseisho 上場申請書 application to list

shinsetsu 新設 new, newly-established

shinsetsu gōben 新設合弁 consolidation (lit. 'merger' 合弁 through 'creation' 新設)

shinshutsu 進出 advance into, make inroads into

kaigai shinshutsu 海外進出 moving into a foreign market

shintaku 信託 trust

baransu-gata tōshi shintaku バランス型投資信託 balanced fund / *giketsu shintaku* 議決信託 voting trust / *kabushiki tōshi shintaku* 株式投資信託 stock investment trust / *kashitsuke shintaku* 貸付信託 loan trust, loan in trust / *kinsen shintaku* 金銭信託 ordinary money trusts, money in trust / *kōsha-sai tōshi shintaku* 公社債投資信託 (open-end) bond investment trust / *kōsha tōshi shintaku* 公社投資信託 (open-end) bond investment trust, public and corporate bond investment trust / *nenkin shintaku* 年金信託 pension trust / *setubi shintaku shōsho* 設備信託証書 equipment trust certificates / *shoken tōshi shintaku* 証券投資信託 securities investment trust / *tokutei kinsen shintaku* 特定金銭信託 special purpose trust / *tōshi shintaku* 投資信託 investment trust / *tōshi shintaku kaisha* (also *tōshi shintaku gaisha*) 投資信託会社 investment trust company / *shintaku kaisha* (also *shintaku gaisha*) 信託会社 trust company / *shintaku keiyaku* 信託契約 indenture, deeds of trust (lit. trust contract) / *shintaku keiyakusho* 信託契約書 indenture

shin'yō 信用 credit

hōkatsu shin'yō hoken 包括信用保険 blanket fidelity bonds / *shin'yō -gai* 信用買い credit purchase, buying future stocks, bull account / *shin'yō hanbai* 信用販売 credit sales (see *shinpan* 信販) / *shin'yō hoken* 信用保険 fidelity bonds / *hōkatsu shin'yō hoken* 包括信用保険 blanket fidelity bonds / *shin'yō kumiai* 信用組合 trust fund / *shin'yō torihiki* 信用取引 margin trading

shisan 資産 assets

genkin shisan kachi 現金資産価値 cash assets value / *genmō shisan* 減耗資産 wasting assets / *ippan shisan* 一般資産 general assets / *kokusai shisan un'yō* 国際資産運用 international asset management / *kōtei shisan* 固定資産 fixed assets, fixed property, capital assets / *kōtei shisan baikyaku* 固定資産売却 sale of capital assets / *kōteki shisan* 公的資産 public assets / *Zenba wa kōteki shisan, tōshi shintaku ga ōgata kabu ni kai o ire shikkari shita tenkai datta ga...* 前場は公的資産、投資信託が大型株に買いを入れしゃっかりした展開だったが... The morning session showed a hiccup in buying large-capital stock by public assets and investment trusts, but... / *mukei shisan* 無形資産 intangible assets / *ryūdō shisan* 流動資産 liquid assets, current assets / *shō kyaku shisan* 償却資産 depreciable assets / *shōmi ryūdō shisan* 正味流動資産 net current assets, working capital / *shōmi tōza shisan-* 正味当座資産 net quick assets / *shōmō shisan* 消耗資産 working assets, depleting assets / *tanaoroshi shisan* 棚卸資産 stock at hand, inventories, working assets / *tōza shisan* 当座資産 quick assets, current assets / *un'yō shisan* 運用資産 assets / *yūkei kōtei shisan* 有形固定資産 tangible fixed assets / *yūkei shisan* 有形資産 tangible assets / *shisan kachi* 資産価値 assets value / *shisan un'yō* 資産運用 money management / *shisan un'yōsha* 資産運用者 fund manager, 'money men'

shisetsu 施設 facilities, installations
kōgai bōshi shisetu muke saiken 公害防止施設向け債券 pollution control bonds (lit. 'bond' 債券 'for' 向け 'pollution' 公害 'prevention' 防止 'installations' 施設)

shishū 支収 balance (of income and expenditure)

shishutsu 支出 expenditure, expenses, outlay
haitō shishutsu 配当支出 dividend requirements / *zaimu-jō no shishutsu* 財務上の支出 financial expenses

shisū 指数 index
kabuka shisū 株価指数 share price index, stock price index / *kouri bukka shisū* 小売物価指数 retail price index / *shōhisha bukka shisū* 消費者物価指数 consumer price index

shitamawaru 下回る be lower than, be less than

shitei 指定 specification
shitei sareta nedan 指定された値段 specified price

*shiwaku 思惑 misreading for *omowaku*

shogakakari 諸掛かり expenses

shōgyō 商業 commerce, mercantile
as a category of equities / *shōgyō tegata* 商業手形 commercial paper

shōheki 障壁 barrier
yunyū shōheki 輸入障壁 import barrier

shōhi 消費 consumption
shōhisha 消費者 consumer (*yūzā* ユーザー is also used, typically in reference to the industrial consumer of a commodity) / *shōhisha bukka shisū* 消費者物価指数 consumer price index

shōhin 商品 commercial product
  kin'yū shōhin 金融商品 financial instrument

sho-hiyō 諸費用 charges

shō kan 償還 redemption, maturity
  renzoku shōkan hō shiki 連続償還方式 serial repayment method / *renzoku shōkan saiken* 連続償還債券 serial bond / *shōkan-ji* 償還時 time of redemption / *shōkan saeki bun* 償還差益分 accretion, accumulation / *shōkan saiken* 償還債券 redemption / *renzoku shōkan saiken* 連続償還債券 serial bond

shōkei 小計 sub-total

shōken 証券 bond certificate, issue, security
  hakkō shōken 発行証券 issue / *hi-jōjō shōken* 非上場証券 unlisted securities / *hi-tōroku shōken* 非登録証券 unregistered security / *hoshō shōken* 保証証券 a guaranteed issue / *hoyū shōken* 保有証券 investment portfolio / *jōi shōken* 上位証券 senior issue / *jōjō shōken* 上場証券 listed security / *jun-ōte shōken kaisha* (also *jun-ōte shoken gaisha*) 準大手証券会社 second-tier securities house / *kai shōken* 下位証券 junior issue / *kakutei ritsuki shōken* 確定利付き証券 fixed-interest security / *kōnin shōken anaristo* 公認証券アナリスト chartered financial analyst (CFA) / *menjo shōken* 免除証券 exempt security / *Ōshu Yotaku Shōken* 欧州預託証券 European Depositary Receipts (EDR) / *ōte shōken kaisha* (also *ōte shōken gaisha*) 大手証券会社 first-tier securities house / *ritsuki shōken* 利付き証券 with-interest security / *ryūtsū shōken* 流通証券 negotiable instrument / *seifu hakkō yūka shōken* 政府発行有価証券 gilt-edged security / *seifu tanki shōken* 政府短期証券 short-term government security / *shinausu shōken* 品薄証券 narrow-market security / *tanki shōken* 短期証券 short-term security / *teitō shōken* 抵当証券 mortgage (pass-through) certificate, mortgage (securities) / *Tōkyō Shōken Torihikisho* (also *Tōkyō Shōken Torihikijo*) 東京証券取引所 Tokyo Stock Exchange / *tōroku shōken* 登録証券 registered security / *yūka shōken* 有価証券 stocks and bonds, negotiable securities / *yūka shōken torihiki zei* 有価証券取引税 transfer tax / *shōken bunseki* 証券分析 security analysis / *shōken gyōsha* 証券業者 broker / *shōken hoyū-daka* 証券保有高 dealer's position (lit. 'volume'高 of 'securities' 証券 'held' 保有) / *shōken tanpo* 証券担保 security / *shōken tanpo-tsuki saiken* 証券担保付き債券 collateral trust bond / *Shōken Torihiki Iinkai* 証券取引委員会 US Securities and Exchange Commission / *shōken torihiki kōza* 証券取引口座

account in securities / *shōken torihikisho* (also *shōken torihikijo*) 証券取引所 securities exchange / *shōken torihiki zei* 証券取引税 transfer tax / *shōken tōshi shintaku* 証券投資信託 securities investment trust

shokku ショック shock
oiru shokku オイル・ショック oil crisis

shokōgyō 商工業 industrials
as a category of equities /*shōkō kaigisho* (also *shōkō kaigijo*) 商工会議所 chamber of commerce and industry

shōko-ki 証拠金 margin, down-payment

shokuhin 食品 foodstuffs (as a category of equities)

shōkyaku 償却 depreciation, repayment, redemption
genka shōkyaku 減価償却 depreciation / *genka shōkyaku hikiate-kin* 減価償却引当金 allowance for depreciation, depreciation reserve / *kaiire shōkyaku* 買い入れ償却 repayment by purchase / *saimu waribiki shōkyaku* 債務割引償却 amortization of discount on funded debt / *waribiki shōkyaku* 割引償却 amortization of discount / *shōkyaku shisan* 償却資産 depreciable assets

shōmi 正味 net
shōmi ryūdō shisan 正味流動資産 net current assets, working capital / *shōmi tōza shisan* 正味当座資産 net quick assets

shōmō 消耗 working
shōmō shisan 消耗資産 working assets, liquid assets

shōsha 商社 trading house

shōsho 証書 certificate, instrument
besshi no jōto shōsho 別紙の譲渡証書 detached assignment / *jōto shōsho* 譲渡証書 assignment certificate / *kariire shōsho* 借入証書 loan certificate / *kenri shōsho* 権利証書 warrant (stock purchase warrant) / *ritsuki shōsho* 利付き証書 interest-bearing certificate / *setsubi shintaku shōsho* 設備信託証書 equipment trust certificate

*shō-ugoki 小動き misreading for *kougoki*

shoyū 所有 hold, own

shoyū-ken 所有権 ownership, proprietorial right, proprietorship / *shoyū sha* 所有者 holder, owner / *saiken shoyū sha* 債券所有者 bondholder / *saimu shoyū sha* 債務所有者 (also *saimusha* 債務者) debtor

shūeki 収益 earnings, profits

eigyō shūeki 営業収益 operating profits / *kabuka shūeki ritsu* 株価収益率 price-earnings ratio (PER) / *kō-shūeki o ageru* 高収益を上げる make fast earnings, earn high profits / *miryoku-teki na shūeki* 魅力的な収益 attractive profit / *shūeki ritsu* 収益率 price-earnings ratio (PER) / *shūeki-ryoku* 収益力 earning power / *shūeki-sei* 収益性 profitability / *Shūeki-sei no men de wa, suimen kara kao o dashi iki ga dekiru yō ni natta teido de, fuyō made okonatte inai to sareru* 収益性の面では、水面から顔を出し息が出来る様になった程度で、浮揚まで行なっていないとされる In respect of profitability, manufacturers are now able to keep their heads above water, if not exactly to emerge onto dry land / *shūeki shasai* 収益社債 income bond, adjustment bond

shūkka 出荷 shipments

shukushō 縮小 shrink, narrow

ōpun kinri to tegata rēto no kakakusa ga shukushō shite kita オープン金利と手形レートの価格差が縮小して来た Differentials between open rates and bill rates have narrowed

shūnyū 収入 income

shurui 種類 class (of stock)

shūryō 終了 close

tachiai shūryō 立会い終了 close of trading / *tachiai shūryō -ji* 立会い終了時 close of trading

shuryoku kabu 主力株 blue-chip stock, leading shares

shūsai 州債 state issues (US)

shūsei 修正 revision, amendment

jōhō shūsei 上方修正 upward revision / *kahō shūsei* 下方修正 downward revision / *shihon shūsei* 資本修正 reconsider

shūshi 終始 maintaining a tone until close
Shijō wa uri-kichō de shūshi shita 市場は売り基調で終始した The market maintained an underlying bearish tone throughout the day

shusshi 出資 capital subscription
shusshi-bun 出資分 share capital

shussho 出所 source, authority
also *shutten* 出典 or *dedokoro* 出所 / Usually found at the bottom of a table or chart crediting the source of the statistics

shutten 出典 source, authority
also *shussho* 出所 or *dedokoro* 出所 / Usually found at the bottom of a table or chart crediting the source of the statistics

shuyō 主要 main, leading
shuyō-koku 主要国 leading country

sōba 相場 market price
Rondon gen'yu supotto shijō no Hokkai Burento sōba wa kougoki ロンドン原油スポット市場の北海ブレント相場は小動き North Sea Brent crude oil prices rose slightly on the London spot market / *kaigai sōba* 海外相場 overseas markets / *madoguchi sōba* 窓口相場 over-the-counter rates / *ōrai sōba* 往来相場 rise-and-fall market / *sōba kakaku* 相場価格 market price / *sōba-shi* 相場師 speculator, stock-jobber / *nomi-koi sōba-shi* 飲みこい相場師 bucket-shop operator, bucketeer / *sōba sōsa* 相場操作 market manipulation

sochi 措置 measure
Teitō ni yori hoshō sarete ita kariire-kin no shiharai o kyōsei suru hōteki sochi 抵当により保証されていた借り入れ金の支払いを強制する法的措置 The legal process of enforcing payment of a debt secured by a mortgage

sōgaku 総額 total value
jika sōgaku 時価総額 total value at market price

sōgo 相互 mutual
kaisha sōgo-kan no kanjō 会社相互間の勘定 inter-company accounts / *sōgo ginkō* 相互銀行 mutual savings bank / *sōgo kakekin* 相互掛け金 instalment savings

sōgō 総合 comprehensive, integrated (accounts)
FT hyakushu sōgō kabuka shisū FT百種総合株価指数 FT-SE 100 index /
sōgō ginkō 総合銀行 universal bank, do-all bank / *sōgō keizai taisaku* 総合
経済対策 comprehensive economic measures, package of emergency economic
measures / *sōgō kōza* 総合口座 general accounts / *sō-hakkō* 総発行 total
issue / *sō -hakkō kabushiki* 総発行株式 total issued stock

*sōhan 窓販 misreading for *madohan*

sōkai 総会 general meeting
kabunushi sōkai 株主総会 shareholders' general meeting / *sōkaiya* 総会屋 a
shareholding agent who disrupts general meetings for extortion

sōkan 相関 correlation
sōkan keisū 相関係数 correlation coefficient / *kinri to kabuka no sōkan
keisū* 金利と株価の相関係数 the correlation coefficient between interest rates
and share prices

sokoire 底入れ bottoming out, hitting bottom

son 損 loss
hyōka son 評価損 evaluation loss / *son'eki* 損益 profit or loss / *rinji son'eki
kōmoku* 臨時損益項目 non-recurrent item (of profit and loss) / *son'eki kanjō*
損益勘定 income account, profit and loss account / *son'eki keisansho* 損益計
算書 income statement / *songai* 損害 damage, harm, loss / *songai hoken* 損害
保険 non-life insurance

sonshitsu 損失 loss
gūhatsu sonshitsu 偶発損失 contingency / *gūhatsu sonshitsu tsumitate-kin*
偶発損失積立金 contingency reserve / *rinji sonshitsu* 臨時損失 non-recurrent
deduction

*sora-torihiki 空取引 misreading for *kara-torihiki*

*sorauri 空売り misreading for *karauri*

sōsa 操作 manipulation
antei sōsa 安定操作 stabilizing operation, stabilizing transaction / *kabuka
sōsa* 株価操作 (share) manipulation / *pūru-sei kumiai sōsa* プール制組合操
作 pool operation / *sōba sōsa* 相場操作 market manipulation

sōsai 総裁 governor
Nichigin sōsai 日銀総裁 governor of the Bank of Japan

sōsai 相殺 offset, compensation, compensating
also, though less frequently *sōsatsu* / *sōsai kanzei* 相殺関税 compensating; compensation duties, countervailing duties; tariff

sōsatsu 相殺 see *sōsai*

sō-seisan 総生産 gross product
kokumin sō-seisan 国民総生産 gross national product (GNP)

sō-shūeki 総収益 gross revenue

sō-uriage daka 総売上高 gross sales

sueoku 据え置く be deferred, non-callable, non-redeemable
Kōru mujōken-mono rēto wa zenshūmatsu-hi kawarazu no 4.0 pāsento (dashite) ni sueokareta コール無条件ものレートは前週末比変わらずの 4%(出し手)に据え置かれた The rate for unconditional call loans was 4.0% selling, unchanged from the previous weekend, and deferred

suii 推移 shift, change
推移 is often present in the titles of statistical tables and charts, meaning 'changes' (e.g. in imports levels), 'past, present and future' statistics (e.g. of land prices), but a translation of the term 推移 is generally redundant / *FT-hyakushu wa zenmen-daka de suii shite iru* FT百種は全面高で推移している Prices of stocks on the FT-SE 100 index are rising across-the-board

suijun 水準 level
kō-suijun 高水準 high level

suisan 水産 marine products
suisan kōgyō 水産鉱業 fisheries & mining (as a category of equities)

suisatsu 推察 infer
...kakaku no agarisugi to, diirā-suji ni yoru urihikae to ni yoru mono de aru to suisatsu suru 価格の上がり過ぎと、ディーラー筋による売り控えとによるものであると推察する ...probably due to excessive price rises, dealers' reluctance to sell and so on

suisu スイス Switzerland
Suisu furan スイス・フラン Swiss franc

suitei 推定 estimate

suji 筋 circles, quarters
omowaku-suji 思惑筋 speculative interests / *seifu-suji* 政府筋 government circles / *tōki-suji* 投機筋 speculative groups

supein スペイン Spain
Supein 100 peseta スペイン100ペセタ 100 Spanish pesetas

supotto スポット spot
supotto shijō スポット市場 spot market / *gen'yu supotto shijō* 原油スポット市場 crude (oil) spot market

sure-sure すれすれ having a close shave, pass by, skim (the surface of the water) / *saisan sure-sure* 採算すれすれ barely profitable (採算 commercial profitability)

susono 裾野 base
lit. 'foothills of a mountain' /*Juyō no susono ga ichidanto kakudai shi...* 需要の裾野が一段と拡大し... The base of demand expanded much more...

suwappu スワップ swap

T

tachiai 立会い session, attendance
tachiai kaishi 立会開始 opening of market / *tachiai shūryō* 立会終了 close of trading / *tachiaiba* 立会場 (trading) floor

tagaku 多額 large sum, large amount
tagaku nōzeisha 多額納税者 upper-bracket taxpayer

Tai タイ Thailand

Tai-bātsu タイ・バーツ the Thai baht

tai- 対 for, vis-a-vis
tai-kokyaku 対顧客 for the customer / *tai-kokyaku kakaku* 対顧客価格 customer price / *tai-Nichi* 対日 with regard to Japan / *tai-Nichi tsūshō seisaku* 対日通商政策 trade and industry policies with regard to Japan / *Kin jigane tentō kakaku (tai kakuaku- 1 guramu)* 金地金店頭価格(対顧客 - 1 グラム) Gold bullion OTC (over- the-counter) price (customer price per gramme) / *tai-zennen-hi* 対前年比 year-on-year (YOY) change (lit. 'compare' 比 to the 'previous year' 前年)

taiki 待機 be on alert, watch and wait
taiki kikan 待機期間 cooling-off period, waiting period

tairyō 大量 large quantity
tairyō-gyoku torihiki 大量玉取引き block transaction

taisaku 対策 countermeasure
kinkyū keizai taisaku 緊急経済対策 emergency economic measures, package of emergency economic measures / *zeikin taisaku* 税金対策 tax purpose

taisei 大勢 general situation, current tide
tsuyoki ga taisei o shimeru 強気が大勢を占める the bulls dominate the general trend

taishaku 貸借 debit and credit, lending and borrowing, loan
taishaku taishō hyō 貸借対照表 balance sheet

taishō 対照 contrast, reference
taishaku taishō hyō 貸借対照表 balance sheet

Taiwan 台湾 Taiwan
Taiwan-doru 台湾ドル Taiwan dollar

taka 高 high, amount, quantity, volume
(often -*daka* in compounds) *en-daka* 円高 the high yen, appreciation of the yen, the strong yen / *saki-daka* 先高 future rise / *saki-daka-kan* 先高感 anticipation of a future rise / *shōken hoyū-daka* 証券保有高 a dealer's position / *uriage-daka* 売上高 (volume of) sales

tanaoroshi 棚卸し stock-taking
 lit. 'taking down' 卸し from the 'shelves' 棚 / *tanaoroshi shisan* 棚卸し資産 inventories, stock in hand, working assets

tandoku gyōseki 単独業績 parent company results

***tankabu 端株** misreading for *hakabu*

tan'i 単位 lot, unit
 tan'i kabu 単位株 round lot, full lot / *torihiki tan'i* 取引単位 trading lot, trading unit

tanki 短期 short term
 tanki kokusai 短期国債 short-term government bonds / *tanki kin'yū shijō* 短期金融市場 money market (c.f. *chōki shihon torihiki shijō* 長期資本取引市場 capital market) / *tanki shō ken* 短期証券 short-term security / *seifu tanki shōken* 政府短期証券 short-term government security

tanpo 担保 collateral, mortgage, security
 mu-tanpo 無担保 without collateral, unsecured / *mu-tanpo kashitsuke* 無担保貸付け straight loan / *mu-tanpo kashitsuke-kin* 無担保貸付け金 unsecured loan / *shōken tanpo* 証券担保 security / *tanpo-tsuki* 担保付き with collateral, mortgaged, with security / *fudōsan tampotsuki saiken* 不動産担保付き債券 debenture (see *fudōsan* 不動産) / *shōken tanpo-tsuki saiken* 証券担保付き債券 collateral trust bond / *tanpo-tsuki saiken* 担保付き債券 mortgage bond

tanri 単利 simple interest

tanshi 短資 short-term loan, call loan dealer
 tanshi kaisha (also *tanshi gaisha*) 短資会社 short-term credit company, money market dealer

tataku 叩く bear the market, undersell
 see *uri tataki* 売り叩き

tegata 手形 cheque, bill
 hyōshi tegata 表紙手形 cover bill / *kaiope tegata* 買いオペ手形 buying operation bill, paper, draft / *kawase tegata* 為替手形 bill of exchange / *nigawase tegata* 荷為替手形 exchange bill / *shōgyō tegata* 商業手形

commercial paper / *yakusoku tegata* 約束手形 promissory note / *tegata kōkansho* (also *tegata kōkanjo*) 手形交換所 clearing house / *tegata rēto* 手形レート bill rate / *tegata waribiki* 手形割引き discount bill / *tegata torihiki* 手形取引き trading in bills

teichō 低調 thin, sluggish, dull
Tegata torihiki wa teichō de... 手形取引きは低調で... Bill trading was thin...

teigaku 低額 small amount

teigakuhō 定額法 constant dollar plan

teigakumen 低額面 low par value
teigakumen kabushiki 低額面株式 low par value stock

teii 低位 low-priced
teii kabu 低位株 low-priced stock, lesser grade stock / *teika* 低下 lowering / *teiri yūshi* 低利融資 low interest financing / *kinri teika* 金利低下 lowering in interest rates

teikan 定款 articles of association

teiki 定期 fixed period
teiki tsumikin 定期積金 instalment savings / *teiki yokin* 定期預金 term deposit, fixed deposit / *teiki-teki* 定期的 regular / *teiki-teki tōshi* 定期的投資 regular investment

teimei 低迷 depression, stagnancy, dullness, levelling off
teiraku 低落 decline, slump

teiri 低利 low interest
teiri-sai 低利債 low interest bond

teishutsu 提出 presenting, filing
teishutsu-bi 提出日 filing date

teitō 抵当 pledge, mortgage
teitō ni yori hoshō sareta kariire kin 抵当により保証された借り入れ金 debt secured by a mortgage / *tochi daikin no jōtoteitō* 土地代金の譲渡抵当 purchase money mortgage / *teitōken* 抵当権 mortgage / *teitōken no jikkō* 抵

当権の実行 implementation of mortgage, foreclosure / *teitō setteisha* 抵当設定者 mortgager / *teitō shōken* 抵当証券 mortgage (pass-through) certificate, mortgage (securities)

tekihō 適法 lawful, legal
tekihō tōshi 適法投資 legal investment

tekisei 適正 appropriate
tekisei kabuka han'i 適正株価範囲 intrinsic range, optimum range

tekkō 鉄鋼 steel
tekkō kabu 鉄鋼株 steel stock / *tekkō kinzoku* 鉄鉱金属 steel & metals (as a category of equities) / *Tekkō nado ōgata kabu ga kenchō de...* 鉄鋼など大型株が堅調で... Steel and other large capital stocks were firm

teko テコ leverage, gearage
Kaisha wa teko no sayō o ōkiku riyō shite iru 会社はテコの作用を大きく利用している The company is highly geared / *teko kabu* テコ株 leverage stock / *teko sayō* テコ作用 leverage

tekunikaru anarisuto テクニカル・アナリスト technical analyst

tenkan 転換 convert, shift
tenkan shasai 転換社債 convertible bond, convertible debenture, mezzanine money

tenpo 店舗 shop
ōgata kouri tenpo 大型小売店舗 large retail store

tentō 店頭 shop
tentō kakaku 店頭価格 OTC (over-the-counter) price / *kin jigane tentō kakaku (tai-kokyaku -1 guramu)* 金地金店頭価格 (対顧客 - 1 グラム) Gold bullion OTC price (customer price per gramme) / *tentō shijō* 店頭市場 over-the-counter (OTC) market / *tentō torihiki* 店頭取引き over-the-counter transaction (see also *madohan* 窓販)

tesūryō 手数料 brokerage, commission, load
hanbai tesūryō 販売手数料 selling concessions / *hikiuke kanji tesūryō* 引受幹事手数料 managing fees / *hikiuke tesūryō* 引受け手数料 underwriting fees, underwriting spread / *itaku tesūryō* 委託手数料 brokerage commission /

kotei tesūryō 固定手数料 fixed commission

tetsuzuki 手続き procedure
kessai tetsuzuki 決済手続き settlement procedure

tobashi トバシ window-dressing schemes with loss-making accounts

toboshii 乏しい poor, scant
shinki zairyō ni toboshii 新規材料に乏しい lacking in fresh incentives

tochi 土地 land
tochi daikin 土地代金 money for land / *tochi daikin jōto teitō* 土地代金譲渡抵当 purchase money mortgage

todokeide 届け出 notice, statement
tōroku todokeide 登録届け出 registration statement

tōjitsu 当日 on that day, the appointed day
tōjitsu torihiki 当日取引き cash delivery

tōkei 統計 statistics
bōeki tōkei 貿易統計 trade statistics

tōki 投機 speculation
tōkika 投機家 speculator, stockjobber / *tōki-suji* 投機筋 speculative groups / *tōki-teki* 投機的 speculative

tokkin 特金 tokkin funds
investment funds favoured by corporate and institutional investors

tokubetsu 特別 special
tokubetsu maruyū 特別マル優 small amount public bond investment exemption / *tokurei kokusai* 特例国債 special bond

tokutei 特定 specific
tokutei kinsen shintaku 特定金銭信託 special purpose trusts

tonaeru 唱える quote
Yobine wa hachi-bun-no-ichi doru no nekizami de tonaerareru 呼び値は8分の1ドルの値刻みで唱えられる Bids and offers are made (quoted) in

99

variations of 1/8 of $1 per share

toppa 突破 breaking through (barrier of)

torihiki 取引き trading, dealing, traffic

ippan kokyaku torihiki shijō 一般記顧客取引市場 outside market, retail market / *kara torihiki* 空取引き wash sales, fictitious transaction / *kikan tōshika torihiki* 機関投資家取引き trading by institutional investors / *kitsume no torihiki* きつめの取引き fairly stringent trading / *kōsei torihiki kisoku* 公正取引規則 rule for fair conduct / *shinyō torihiki* 信用取引き margin trading / *Shōken Torihiki Iinkai* 証券取引委員会 US Securities and Exchange Commission / *shōken torihiki koza* 証券取引口座 account in securities / *Shōken Torihiki Shingikai* 証券取引審議会 Securities Exchange Council / *shōken torihiki zei* 証券取引税 transfer tax / *tegata torihiki* 手形取引き trading in bills / *tentō torihiki* 店頭取引き over-the-counter transaction / *tairyō-gyoku torihiki* 大量玉取引き block transaction / *tōjitsu torihiki* 当日取引き cash delivery / *torihiki tan'i* 取引単位 trading lot, trading unit

torihikisho 取引所 trading place, trading floor, exchange

also *torihikijo* / *shōken torihikisho* 証券取引所 stock exchange / *tōroku menjo torihikisho* 登録免除取引所 exempt stock exchange / *tōroku torihikisho* 登録取引所 registered exchange

torikeshi 取消し cancel

torikeshi chūmon 取り消し注文 cancel order

torishimariyaku 取締役 director

tōroku 登録 registering, entry, record

tōroku menjo torihikisho (also *tōroku menjo torihikijo*) 登録免除取引所 exempt stock exchange / *tōroku shōken* 登録証券 registered security / *tōroku todoke-sho* 登録届け書 registration certificate / *tōroku torihikisho* (also *tōroku torihikijo*) 登録取引所 registered exchange / *tōrokunin* 登録人 registrar / *kabushiki tōrokunin* 株式登録人 registrar of stock

toshi 都市 city

toshi ginkō 都市銀行 city bank

tōshi 投資 investing, investment

kabushiki tōshi shintaku 株式投資信託 investment trust / *kappu tōshi* 割賦

投資 instalment investment / *kōsha-sai tōshi shintaku* 公社債投資信託 (open end) bond investment trust, public and corporate bond investment trust / *pōtoforio tōshi* ポートフォリオ投資 portfolio management, investment management / *setsubi tōshi* 設備投資 capital investment (in plant and equipment) / *shōken tōshi shintaku* 証券投資信託 securities investment trust / *teiki-teki tōshi* 定期的投資 regular investment / *tekihō tōshi* 適法投資 legal investment / *tōshika* 投資家 investor / *kikan tōshika torihiki* 機関投資家取引き trading by institutional investors / *ippan tōshika* 一般投資家 individual investor, the investing public / *tōshi komongyō* 投資顧問業 investment advisory service / *tōshi shintaku* 投資信託 investment trust (often shortened to *tōshin* 投信) / *tōshi shintaku kaisha* (also *tōshi shintaku gaisha*) 投資信託会社 investment trust company / *tōshin* 投信 investment trust, mutual fund (short for *tōshi shintaku* 投資信託)

tōsho 当初 initial
tōsho mikomi 当初見込み initial forecast

Tōshō 東証 Tokyo Stock Exchange
short for *Tōkyō Shōken Torihikisho / Torihikijo* 東京証券取引所

tōza 当座 account
shōmi tōza shisan 正味当座資産 net quick assets / *tōza hiritsu* 当座比率 quick ratio, acid test ratio, quick assets ratio / *tōza shisan* 当座資産 quick assets, current assets / *tōza yokin* 当座預金 current deposit, current account

tsūchi 通知 notice, notification
tsūchi yokin 通知預金 notice deposit

tsuika 追加 additional, postscript
tsuika-teki 追加的 additional / *tsuika-teki na sōgō keizai taisaku* 追加的な総合経済対策 additional package of comprehensive economic measures

*tsuishō 追証 misreading for *oishō*

tsūjō 通常 ordinary, conventional

tsūka 通貨 currency
tsūka kyōkyūryō 通貨供給量 money supply / *tsūka shijō* 通貨市場 currency market / *Ōshū tsūka shijō* 欧州通貨市場 European currency markets, Euro-dollar market

tsukeru 付ける reach

En wa yoritsuki chokugo kara 128-en chōdo o tsuketa 円は寄り付き直後
から128円ちょうどを付けた Shortly after the market opened the yen reached
exactly 128 to the dollar

tsūki 通期 on an annualized basis

lit. 'passing through', 'throughout' 通 the 'financial term' 期

*tsukine 着値 misreading of *chakune*

tsumiageru 積み上げる to accumulate

*Yūtanpo kōru mo shikin no dashite ga junbi yokin o tsumiageta tame,
kitsume no torihiki datta* 有担保コールも資金の出手が準備預金を積み上
げた為、きつめの取引きだった Trading in collateralled calls was fairly
stringent due to the accumulation of reserve deposits on the part of providers of
funds

tsumikin 積み金 savings

teiki tsumikin 定期積み金 instalment savings

tsumitate 積立て reserve

tsumitate en 積立て円 reserved yen / *tsumitate-kin* 積立て金 reserved fund,
appropriation of surplus for reserves

tsunagi つなぎ hedging

tsūsan 通産 trade and industry

short for *tsūshō sangyō* 通商産業 trade and industry / *tsūsan seisaku* 通産
政策 policies on trade and industry / *tsūsan-shō* 通産省 Ministry of
International Trade and Industry (MITI), short for *Tsūshō Sangyō Shō* 通商産
業省 MITI

tsūshin 通信 telecommunications

un'yu tsūshin 運輸通信 transport & telecommunications (as a category of
equities)

tsūshō 通商 international trade

tsūshō seisaku 通商政策 international trade policies / *kyōtsū tsūshō seisaku*
共通通商政策 common international trade policy / *EC wa tai-Nichi tsūshō
seisaku o kyōka shite kite iru* EC は対日通商政策を強化して来ている

The EC has conventionally strengthened its trade policies with regard to Japan

tsuyoi 強い strong, bullish
tsuyofukumi 強含み strong tone / *tsuyofukumu* 強含む edge up / *tsuyoki* 強気 bullishnesss, strong tone / *Tsuyoki ga taisei o shimeru* 強気が大勢を占める Bullishness dominates the general trend

U

*uebanare 上放れ misreading for *uwabanare*

*uemawaru 上回る misreading for *uwamawaru*

*uene 上値 misreading for *uwane*

*uesaya 上鞘 misreading for *uwezaya*

uezaya 上鞘 higher in quotation

ugokiyasusa 動き安さ volatility
kakaku no ugokiyasusa 価格の動き安さ volatility in stock

ukemodoshi-ken 受け戻し権 redemption right

ukemodosu 受け戻す redeem

ukewatashi 受け渡し delivery, transfer
ukewatashi seido 受け渡し制度 five-day delivery plan

umare-ne 生れ値 opening price

umeru 埋める cover a loss, bury
also *uzumeru*

un'yō 運用 management
kokusai shisan un'yō 国際資産運用 international asset management / *shikin un'yō* 資金運用 money management / *shisan un'yō* 資産運用 money

management / *un'yōsha* 運用者 manager / *shikin un'yōsha* 資金運用者 fund manager, 'money man' / *shisan un'yōsha* 資産運用者 fund manager, 'money man'

un'yō shisan 運用資産 assets

un'yu 運輸 transport

un'yu tsūshin 運輸通信 transport & telecommunications (as a category of equities)

uon ウォン the won

Kankoku-100-uon 韓国100ウォン 100 Korean won

uragaki 裏書き endorsement

uraguchi 裏口 backdoor

uraguchi jōjō 裏口上場 'backdoor listing' (achieved by a non-listed company amalgamating with a listed company)

urazukeru 裏付ける back-up, endorse, evidence

Ittei no manki o motsu shōsho ni yotte urazukerarete iru shihon 一定の満期を持つ証書によって裏付けられている資本 Capital endorsed by a certificate with specific maturity

uri 売り bearish, selling market

uri ni dasu 売りに出す to offer / *uri ni dasareta* 売りに出された offered for sale / *uri ni deru* 売りに出る to offer / *rōbai uri* 狼狽売り blind sale / *uriagari* 売り上がり selling on a rising scale / *uriage* 売り上げ sales / *uriage-daka* 売り上げ高 sales / *uriba* 売り場 place of sales, chance to sell / *uri chūmon* 売り注文 offer / *uridashi* 売り出し secondary offering / *urihikaeru* 売り控える reluctant to sell, slow to sell / *Kakaku ni agarisugi, diirā-suji ni yoru urihikae to ni yoru mono de aru to suisatsu suru* 価格の上がり過ぎ、ディーラー筋による売り控えとによるものであると推察する ...probably due to excessive prices rises, dealers' reluctance to sell and so on / *uri honzon* 売り本尊 leader of short side (本尊 is an object of devotion which is enshrined in a Buddhist temple as the chief image of the Buddha. By extension, 本尊 is the leader of a group of items) / *urikake* 売り掛け credit sales / *urikake-kin* 売り掛け金 accounts receivable / *urikata* 売り方 seller, bear interests / *urikata hibu* 売り方日歩 seller's per diem rate / *urikata katte watashi* 売り方勝手渡し seller's option / *uri-kehai* (also *uri-kewai*) 売り気

配 ask quotation / *uri kichō* 売り基調 an underlying bearish market tone / *urikomi* 売り込み heavy selling, canvassing for sales / *urikoshi* 売り越し net selling, selling on balance / *urikuzushi* 売り崩し bear raid, depressing the market, selling off / *urikuzusu* 売り崩す sell off, bang the market / *urimochi* 売り持ち short position / *urimodoshi* 売り戻し resale / *urimodoshi-ken* 売り戻し権 right to re-sell / *urinaga* 売り長 sellers over, short interest exceeding long stocks / *urinige* 売り逃げ unloading / *urinose* 売り乗せ putting on more / *uritataki* 売り叩き bearing the market, underselling / *urite* 売り手 seller / *uritsuke chūmon* 売り付け注文 selling order / *uritsunagi* 売りつなぎ short sale against the box, shaking out, hedging / *uriyobine* 売り呼び値 asking price, offer

Uōru-gai ウォール街 Wall Street

uwabanare 上放れ jump, break away, upside penetration

uwamawaru 上回る surpass, top

uwane 上値 higher price

W

wareru 割れる fall below
zennen ware wa 8-kagetsu renzoku 前年割れは 8 ヶ月連続 This was the eighth month running that (it) dipped below the level of the previous year / *ōdai-ware* 大台割れ falling below the barrier (of e.g. ¥200, with regard to a price previously of e.g. ¥201 or above)

waribiki 割引き discount
waribiki de uru 割引きで売る sell at a discount / *waribiki kinyū sai* 割引金融債 discount bank debenture / *waribiki kokusai* 割引国債 discount government bond / *waribiki ritsu* 割引率 discount rate / *waribiki shōkyaku* 割引償却 amortization of discount / *saimu waribiki shōkyaku* 債務割引償却 amortization of discount on funded debt

waridaka 割高 rather high in cost price, rather expensive

waru 割る drop below (the barrier of)

watasu 渡す offer
　tōshika no te ni watasu 投資家の手に渡す offer to investors

watashi 渡し delivery
　torihiki no chūshin de aru shichigatsu-watashi 取引きの中心である７月渡し the key July delivery

Y

yaku- 約 approximately
　yaku-roppyaku-oku-en 約600億円 'approximately ¥60 bn'

yakuhin kabu 薬品株 pharmaceutical stock

yakuin 役員 officer

yakujō 約定 arrangements, bargain, stipulation

yakusoku 約束 promise
　yakusoku tegata 約束手形 promissory note

yasu 安 fall
　lit. 'cheap', 'low' / *sanpatsu yasu* 散発安 sporadic falls

yaya やや somewhat

yobine 呼び値 bids and offers, nominal price
　kai yobine 買い呼び値 bidding price

yo 予 estimate, forecast, prediction
　short for *yosoku* 予測 / *Yo* 予 is put after column headings where the figures are predicted, as opposed to actual results *jisseju* 実績 (i.e. for the past and previous fiscal years) and *mikomi* 見込み prospects (i.e. for the present fiscal year)

yōgyō 窯業 ceramics industry

gomu yōgyō ゴム窯業 rubber & ceramics (as a category of equities)

yojō 余剰 surplus
shikin yojō jiai 資金余剰地合い overall pattern of an excess of funds

yokin 預金 deposit, bank account
futsū yokin 普通預金 ordinary account / *jisshitsu yokin* 実質預金 real deposit / *nōzei junbi yokin* 納税準備預金 deposit for tax payments / *ryōdate yokin* 両建預金 compensating balance / *teiki yokin* 定期預金 term deposit, fixed deposit / *tōza yokin* 当座預金 current deposit, current account / *tsūchi yokin* 通知預金 notice deposit

yoritsuku 寄り付く open
En wa Tōkyō no owari-ne yori yaya takaku yoritsuita 円は東京の終り値よりやや高く寄り付いた The yen opened somewhat higher than the Tokyo closing price

yosan 予算 budget
hosēi yosan 補正予算 supplementary budget

yosoku 予測 forecast
In tables, often *yo* 予. *Yo* 予 is put after column headings where the figures are predicted, as opposed to actual results *Jiseki* 実績 (i.e. for previous fiscal years) and *mikomi* 見込み prospects (i.e. for the present and subsequent fiscal years)

yōsu 様子 appearance
yōsumi 様子見 wait-and-see, keeping to the sidelines / *Shinki zairyō-busoku de, akinai-usu no naka, shijō wa yōsumikibun ga tsuyoi* 新規材料不足で、商い薄の中、市場は様子見気分が強い Players kept to the sidelines in thin trading caused by a lack of incentives

yotaku 預託 deposit
Ōshu Yotaku Shōken 欧州預託証券 European Depositary Receipts (EDR)

yowai 弱い weak
yowabukumi 弱含み weak tone / *yowafukumu* 弱含む edge down / *yowaki* 弱気 bearish, weak

yoyaku 予約 hedging

yoyū shikin 余裕資金 surplus funds, lee-way

yūbin 郵便 postal service
yūbin chokin 郵便貯金 Post Office savings

*yubine 指値 misreading for *sashine*

yūchi 誘致 attraction
sangyō yūchi muke saiken 産業誘致向け債券 industrial revenue bonds (lit. 'bonds' 債券 'for' 向け the 'attraction' 誘致 of 'industry' 産業)

yuigon 遺言 will
yuigon shikkōsha 遺言執行者 executor

yūka 有価 valuable, negotiable
seifu hakkō yūka shōken 政府発行有価証券 gilt-edged security / *yūka shōken* 有価証券 stocks and bonds, negotiable securities / *yūka shōken torihiki zei* 有価証券取引税 transfer tax

yūkei 有形 tangible
yūkei kōtei shisan 有形固定資産 tangible fixed assets / *yūkei shisan* 有形資産 tangible assets

yunyū 輸入 imports
kinkyū yunyū seigen 緊急輸入制限 safeguards (lit. 'emergency' 緊急 'imports' 輸入 'limits' 制限) / *yunyū isondo* (also *yunyū izondo*) 輸入依存度 rate of dependence on imports / *yunyū shōheki* 輸入障壁 import barrier / *yunyū zōka* 輸入増加 increased imports

yūryō 優良 superior, excellent
yūryō kabu 優良株 blue chips / *yūryō meigara* 優良銘柄 prime issue

yūsen 優先 preference
shinkabu yūsen hikiuke-ken 新株優先引受権 privileged subscription right / *yūsen haitō* 優先配当 stipulated dividend, preferred dividend / *yūsen kabu* 優先株 preferred stock / *ruiseki yūsen kabu* 累積優先株 cumulative preferred stock / *yūsen kabushiki* 優先株式 preferred stock / *sankateki yūsen kabushiki* 参加的優先株式 participating preferred stock / *hisanka-teki yūsen kabushiki* 非参加的優先株式 non-participating preferred stock

yūshi 融資 financing, advance of funds

yusō 輸送 transportation of goods
yusō seimitsu 輸送精密 transport and precision tools (as a category of equities)

yū-tanpo 有担保 collateralled, mortgaged
Yū-tanpo kōru mo shikin no dashite ga junbi-yokin o tsumiageta tame, kitsume no torihiki datta 有担保コールも資金の出手が準備預金を積み上げたため、きつめの取引きだったTrading in collateralled calls was fairly stringent due to the accumulation of reserve deposits on the part of providers of funds

*yūtsū 融通 misreading for *yūzū*

yūzā ユーザー user, consumer
typically in reference to the industrial consumer of a commodity

yūzū 融通 circulation, finance, loan

Z

zaiko 在庫 stocks, inventories
gen'yu zaiko 原油在庫 crude stockpiles / *zaiko chōsei* 在庫調整 inventories adjustment / *zurekomu keiki kaifuku de gensan, zaiko chōsei kyōka e* ずれ込む景気回復で減産、在庫調整強化へ reduced production and inventory adjustment as recovery recedes further / *zaiko-gai* 在庫買い buying-up stocks

zaimu 財務 finances
zaimu dairinin 財務代理人 fiscal agent / *zaimu-jō no shishutsu* 財務上の支出 financial expenses / *zaimu shohyō* 財務諸表 statement

zairyō 材料 incentives, factor, element, material
amami zairyō 甘味材料 sweetener / *hikiage zairyō* 引上げ材料 price-raising factor / *BT ga sōchō ni kō-kessan o happyō shita no mo zentai no sōba no hikiage zairyō to natte iru* BTが早朝に好決算を発表したのも全体の相場の引き上げ材料となっている Traders reacted favourably to the

announcement of good business results by BT / *shinki zairyō* 新規材料 fresh
incentives / *Sōba o sayū suru shinki zairyō ga naku, ne-ugoki wa chiisai*
相場を左右する新規材料がなく、値動きは小さい Prices moved within a
narrow range, reflecting the lack of fresh incentives in the market / *shinki*
zairyō ni toboshii 新規材料に乏しい lacking in fresh incentives / *zairyō*
detsukushi-kan 材料出尽し感 running out of incentives / *Shijō ni wa zairyō*
detsukushi-kan mo ari, neugoki wa chiisai 市場には材料出尽し感もあ
り、値動きは小さい The market ran out of incentives and price changes were
small / *zairyō-nan* 材料難 lack of incentives / *zairyō zandaka* 材料残高
holdings, balance

-zan 残 balance
kariire-zan 借入れ残 debit balance / *zandaka* 残高 balance / *kashikata*
zandaka 残高 credit balance

zaseki 座席 seat on an exchange

zei 税 tax
kabushiki torihiki zei 株式取引税 transfer tax / *zeihiki* 税引き tax-deducted,
after-tax / *zeihiki rieki* 税引き利益 after-tax earnings / *zeikin* 税金 tax /
zeikin taisaku 税金対策 tax purposes / *zeisei* 税制 tax system / *zeisei*
kaikaku 税制改革 tax reforms

zenba 前場 morning market, morning session
Zenba wa kōteki shisan, tōshi shintaku ga ōgata kanu ni kai o ire
shakkari shita tenka datta ga... 前場は公的資産、投資信託が大型株に買
いを入れしっかりした展開だったが... The morning session showed a hiccup
in buying large-capital stock by public assets and investment trusts, but...

zengaku 全額 total amount
zengaku shihon no kogaisha 全額資本の子会社 wholly-owned subsidiary

zengetsu 前月 last month, the previous month
zengetsu-hi 前月比 compared with the previous month

Zenkoku Ginkō Kyōkai Rengōkai 全国銀行協会連合会
Federation of Bankers Associations of Japan

zenmen 全面 across the board
FT-hyakushu wa zenmen-daka de suii shite iru FT百種は全面高で推移し

ている Prices of stocks in the FT-SE index rose across-the-board

zennen 前年 last year, the previous year

zennen-hi 前年比 compared with the previous year, year-on-year (YOY) growth / *zennen ware wa 8-kagetsu renzoku* 前年割れは 8 ヶ月連続 This was the eighth month running that it dipped below the level of the previous year

zenpan 前半 first half, earlier half

127-en dai zenpan 127円台前半 the lower regions of the first half of the ¥127-mark

zenshūmatsu 前週末 the previous weekend

zenshūmatsu-hi 前週末比 compared to the previous weekend (*-hi* 比 'compared with')

zero ゼロ zero, nought, nil

zero kokusai ゼロ国債 zero bonds i.e. authorizations for public works contracts

-zō 増 increase

Kashidashi-kin wa zengetsu-hi 625-oku-en-zō no 219-chō 9,928-oku en datta 貸し出し金は前月比625億円増の219兆9928億円だった The value of loans totalled 219,992.8 billion yen, up 62.5 billion yen month-on-month / *zō eki* 増益 increased profits / *zō hai* 増配 increased dividend / *zō ka* 増加 increase / *yunyū zō ka* 輸入増加 increased imports / zokuraku 続落 continued fall / *zokushin* 続伸 continued rise / *30-nichi no Rondon kabishiki sōba wa zokushin* 30日のロンドン株式相場は続伸 Stock prices continued to rise on the London stock market of 30 August / *zō san* 増産 increased production

zōsen kabu 造船株 shipbuilding stock

zōyo 贈与 donation; presentation

shikin zōyo 資金贈与 donation of funds

zu 図 chart (illustration, statistics etc.)

zurekomu ずれ込む recede, slide further

zurekomu keiki kaifuku de gensan, zaiko chōsei kyōka e ずれ込む景気回復で減産、在庫調整強化へ reduced production and further inventory adjustment as recovery recedes / *zurekomi juyō* ずれ込み需要 demand carry-over, postponed demand

PART TWO

ENGLISH – ROMAJI

A

account	kaikei
	kanjō
	kōza
accounts payable	kaikake-kin
accounts receivable	urikake-kin
accrue	shūeki
accrued depreciation	genka shōkyaku hikiate kin
accrued expense	miharai hiyō
accrued revenue	mi-shūnyū-kin
long-term accrued revenue	chōki maebarai hiyō
accrued income	mishū shūeki
accrued amount	miharai-kin
accrued amount for facilities	setsubi kankei miharai-kin
accrued tax	hōjin-zei-tō jūtō-kin
accumulate	ruiseki
	tsumitate
accumulated depreciation	shōkyaku ruikeigaku
accumulated depreciation for intangible asset	yūkei kotei shisan shōkyaku ruikeigaku
accumulated depreciation ratio	ruikei shōkyaku hiritsu
accumulated fund	tsumitate-kin
accumulated fund for dividends	chūkan haitō tsumitate-kin
accumulation system	akyūmurēshion hōshiki

acquisition	akuijishion
	baishū
	gappei
additional	fuka
	tsuika
additional paid-in capital	gakumen chōka-bun
adjustment	chōsei
inventories adjustment	zaiko chōsei
administration	gyōsei
selling, general & admin. cost	hanbai-hi kanri-hi
advance	maewatashi-kin
advance from new equity issue	shin-kabushiki haraikomi-kin
advance received	maeuke-kin
adverse	furieki
	gyaku
	hantai
with no adverse factors	akunuke
adverse factor	aku-zairyō
agent	dairinin
fiscal agent	zaimu dairinin
allowance for depreciation	genka shōkyaku hikiate kin
allowances	kurinobe shisan
	kyūyo
	teate
short-term allowance	tanki hikiate-kin
allowance for bonus	shōyo hikiate kin
American dollar bond	doru-date saiken
American Stock Exchange	Amekkusu
amount	gaku
	ryō
accrued amount	miharai-kin
accrued amount for facilities	setsubi kankei miharai-kin

analysis	bunseki
security analysis	shōken bunseki
analyst	anarisuto
fundamental analyst	fundamentaru anaritsu
annual	nenji
	nenkan
annualized	tsūki
	tsūnen
appraisal	hyōka
appraisal loss from asset	shisan hyōka son
appraisal loss from securities	yūka shōken hyōka son
appraisal profit	hyōka eki
Asian-dollar bond	Ajia darā sai
asset	shisan
appraisal loss from asset	shisan hyōka son
capital assets	kotei shisan
current assets	ryūdō shisan
depreciable assets	shōkyaku taishō shisan
fixed asset	kotei shisan
intangible fixed asset	mukei kotei shisan
quick assets	tōza shisan
tangible fixed asset	yūkei kotei shisan
total asset	shisan gōkei
asset sales	shisan shobun
loss from asset sales	shisan shobun son
profit from asset sales	shisan shobun eki
auction	kyōsō baibai, seri baibai
automobile	jidōsha
	sharyō
automobiles etc. (on balance sheet)	senpaku sharyō unpangu

B

bad	furyō
bad asset	furyō shisan
bad debt	furyō saiken
	kashidaore
reserve for bad debt	kashidaore hikiate-kin
balance	sakaku
	zandaka
balance sheet	taishaku taishō hyō
balanced fund	baransu-gata tōshi shintaku
bankruptcy	hasan
claims provable in bankruptcy	hasan saiken
barrel	bareru
benchmark	benchi māku
	kijunten
	sokutei kijun
bond	shasai
	shōken
Asian-dollar bond	Ajia darā-sai
convertible bond	tenkan shasai
corporate bond	shasai
bond issue	shasai hakkō
bond issue cost	shasai hakkō hi
bond repurchase agreement	gensaki
bond repurchase market	gensaki shijō
book profit	chōbō-jō rieki
borrowing	kariire-kin

long-term borrowing	chōki kariire-kin
short-term borrowing	tanki kariire-kin
bonus	shōyo
allowance for bonus	shōyo hikiate-kin
break-even point	shūshi bunki-ten
	son'eki bunki-ten
brisk	kappatsu
broker	gyōsha
brokerage	itaku baibai
building	biru
	tatemono
bull	aoru
	kaiire
	tsuyofukumu
	tsuyoki
business day	eigyō-jitsu
business report	eigyō hōkokusho
buying	kau
	kōnyū
support buying	ajitsuke
	ajitsuke-gai
buying and selling	baibai
buying order	kaitsuke chūmon

C

cancel order	torikeshi chūmon
capital	shihon
	shisan

additional paid-in capital	gakumen chōka-bun
capital assets	kotei shisan
capital expenditure	setsubi tōshi
capital gain	kyapitaru gein
capital investment	setsubi tōshi
capital market	chōki shihon torihiki shijō
capital reserve	shihon jōyo-kin shihon junbi-kin
carte blanche order	nariyuki chūmon
cash	genbutsu genkin
cash account	genkin kanjō
cash assets value	genkin shisan kachi
cash balance	genkin zandaka
cash bonds	genbutsu sai
cash & deposit	genkin yokin
cash flow	kyasshu-furō
cash holdings	genkin zandaka
cash realisation	genkin-ka
cash trading	genbutsu torihiki
CBI (Confederation of British Industry)	Eikoku Sangyō Renmei
ceiling	atama-uchi
chartered	kōnin
chartered financial analyst	kōnin shōken anarisuto
circular	annaisho
bond circular	boshū annaisho
offering circular	boshū annaisho
claim	seikyū yokyū
claims provable in bankruptcy	hasan saiken hasan saiken kōsei saiken

compensating deposit	buzumi
	ryōdate
common stock	futsū kabu
Confederation of British Industry	Eikoku Sangyō Renmei
convertible bonds	tenkan shasai
construction	kensetsu
construction in progress	kensetsu kari-kanjō
consumer	shōshisha
consumer price index	shōhisha bukka shisū
corporate bond	shasai
cost	daikin
	genka
	hi
	hiyō
bond issue cost	shasai hakkō hi
depreciation cost	genka shōkyaku hi
fixed cost	kotei genka
	kotei hiyō
fixed cost ratio	kotei-hi ritsu
research cost	kaihatsu-hai shiken kenyū-hi
variable cost	hendō-hi
	kahen hiyō
variable cost ratio	hendō-hi ritsu
cost of sales	hanbai hi
	uriage genka
coverage	kabarejji
interest coverage ratio	interesuto kabarejji ritsu
crash	bōraku
creditor	saikensha
crossing order	baikai
crude oil	gen'yu
currency	tsūka

foreign currency	gaika
current	genzai
	ryūdō
	tō-
current assets	ryūdō shisan
current liabilities	ryūdō fusai
current ratio	ryūdō hiritsu
customs	kanzei

D

daylight trading	hibakari akinai
dealer	diirā
dealing	baibai
debenture	fudōsan tampo-tsuki saiken
debt	fusai
	shakkin
bad debt	kashidaore
reserve for bad debt	kashidaore hikiate-kin
debt ratio	fusai hiritsu
debtor	fusaisha
	saimusha
decline	genshō
defer	kurinoberu
	sueoku
deficit	akaji
trade deficit	bōeki akaji
deferred income	maeuke shūeki
degree	do

degree of operating leverage	eigyō teko-ritsu
deposit	yokin
cash & deposit	genkin yokin
foreign currency deposits	gaika yokin
deposit from employee	jūgyōin azukari-kin
depreciable assets	shōkyaku taishō shisan
depreciation	genka shōkyaku
depreciation cost	genka shōkyaku hi
depreciation reserve	genka shōkyaku hikiate kin
development	hatten
	kaihatsu
research & development	kenkyū kaihatsu
research and development expenditure	kenkyū kaihatsu hi
device	debaisu
difference	baratsuki
discount	genka
	waribiki
discount rate	kōtei buai
discretionary order	baibai ichinin chūmon
disparity	baratsuki
disposal	baikyaku
diversification	bunsan
	tayōka
diversified investment	bunsan tōshi
dividend	haitō
	haitō-kin
	shiharai
accumulated fund for dividends	chūkan haitō tsumitate-kin
interest & dividend expense	shiharai risoku waribiki-ryō
dividend received	uketori haitō-kin
dollar	doru

123

dollar cost averaging	doru heikin hō
do-not-reduce order	genka muyō
drop	genshō
	geraku
dull	amai

E

easy	amai
Economic Planning Agency	Keizai Kikaku Chō
employee	jūgyōin
deposit from employee	jūgyōin azukari-kin
enterprise	jigyō
enterprise profit	jigyō rieki
	jigyō shueki
EPA (Economic Planning Agency)	Keizai Kikaku Chō
equipment	sochi
machinery & equipment	kikai sochi
equity	jiko shihon
	kabushiki
advance from new equity issue	shin-kabushiki haraikomi-kin
exchange (rate)	kawase
execution (of an order)	shikkō
expansion	kakudai
rise in trade deficit	bōeki akaji kakudai
expenditure	keihi
	shusshi
capital expenditure	setsubi tōshi

expense	hiyō
	sonshitsu
accrued expense	miharai hiyō
non-operating expense	eigyō-gai hiyō
prepaid expense	maebarai hiyō
special expense	tokubetsu hiyō
export	yushutsu
	yushutsu uriage-daka
external bond	gaikoku sai

F

face value	gakumen
facilities	setsubi
accrued amount for facilities	setsubi kankei miharai-kin
notes payable for facilities	setsubi kankei shiharai tegata
factor	yōin
adverse factor	aku-zairyō
with no adverse factors	akunuke
fall	genshō
	geraku
fast profits	kōshūeki
finance	kin'yū
chartered financial analyst	kōnin shōken anarisuto
financial statement	zaimu shohyō
financing	kin'yū chōtatsu
	kin'yū yūshi
finish	shūryō

finished goods	kakōhin
	seihin
	shōhin
fix	kotei
	settei
fixed asset	kotei shisan
intangible fixed asset	mukei kotei shisan
tangible fixed asset	yūkei kotei shisan
fixed assets to net worth ratio	kotei hiritsu
fixed cost	kotei genka
	kotei-hi
fixed cost ratio	kotei-hi ritsu
fixed liabilities	chōki fusai
	kotei fusai
floating	fudō
floating stock	fudō gyoku
	fudō kabu
floating supply	fudō gyoku
	fudō kabu
flow	furō
price cash-flow ratio	kabuka kyasshu-furō ritsu
foreign bond	gaikoku sai
	gaisai
foreign capital	gaishi
foreign currency	gaika
foreign exchange	gaikoku kawase
foreign exchange market	gaikoku kawase shijō
free	jiyū
free auction market	jiyū kyōsō baibai shijō
fuel	aoru
fund	kikin
accumulated fund	tsumitate-kin
accumulated fund for dividends	chūkan haitō tsumitate-kin

fundamental analyst	fuandamentaru anarisuto
funded debt	chōki fusai

gain	gein
GATT	Gatto
	Kanzei Bōeki Ippan Kyōtei
general	futsū
	ippan
selling, general & admin. cost	hanbai-hi kanri-hi
GNP	kokumin sō-seisan
goods	kakōhin
	seihin
	shōhin
finished goods	shōhin seihin
unfinished goods	han-seihin
gross	sō-
gross national product (GNP)	kokumin sō-seisan
gross profit	sō-rieki
	sō-shūeki
	uriage sō-rieki

H

hiring	chinshaku
holding	hoyū
	shoyū
investment holdings	antei kabu

I

income	shūnyū
accrued income	mishū shūeki
deferred income	maeuke shūeki
indebtedness	fusai
index	shisū
indicator	shisū
industry	gyōkai (industrial circles)
	kōgyō (manufacturing industry)
	sangyō (producing industry)
insolvency	shiharai funō
instalment	bunkatsu-barai
	kappu
unrealized profit of instalment	kappu hanbai mi-jitsugen rieki
instalment investment	kappu tōshi
intangible	mukei

intangible fixed asset	mukei kotei shisan
interest	kinri
	rishi
	risoku
interest coverage ratio	interesuto kabarejji ritsu
interest & dividend expense	shiharai risoku waribiki-ryō
interest received	uketori risoku
	uketori risoku waribiki-ryō
intermediary	chūkai
intermediation	chūkaika
inventory, inventories	tanaoroshi shisan
	zaiko
inventory adjustment	zaiko chōsei
investment	tōshi
capital investment	setsubi tōshi
instalment investment	kappu tōshi
investment holdings	entei kabu
investment securities	tōshi yūka shōken
issue	hakkō
bond issue	shasai hakkō
bond issue cost	shasai hakkō hi

L

land	tochi
money for land	tochi daikin
launch	fumikiru
	hatsubai

lease	chinshaku
	riisu
leased property	riisu bukken
legal	gōhō
	horitsu-jō
legal reserve of retained earnings	rieki junbi-kin
lender	dashite
leverage	tekoritsu
liabilities	fusai
current liabilities	ryūdō fusai
fixed liabilities	kotei fusai
total liabilities & TNW	fusai shihon gōkei
limited order	sashine chūmon
liquidity	ryūdōsei
liquidity ratio	ryūdōsei hiritsu
loan	kashitsuke
long-term loan	chōki kashitsuke-kin
short-term loan	tanki kashitsuke-kin
local	chihō no
local government bond	chihō jichitai sai
	chihō jichitai saimu shōken
long-term	chōki
	chō-kikan
long-term accrued revenue	chōki maebarai hiyō
long-term borrowing	chōki kariire-kin
long-term government bonds	chōki ritsuki kokusai
long-term loan	chōki kashitsuke-kin
long-term note payable	chōki shiharai tegata
long-term reserve for debt	chōki hikiate-kin
lose ground	geraku
loss	son
	sonshitsu

appraisal loss from asset	shisan hyōka son
profit & loss	son'eki
profit & loss statement	son'eki keisansho
loss from sales of asset	shisan shobun son
loss from sales of property	yūkei kotei shisan shobun son

M

machinery	kikai
machinery & tools	kiki
margin	genkai
marginal cost of production	genkai seisan kosuto
marginal profit	genkai rieki
	genki rijun
marginal profit ratio	genkai rieki-ritsu
mark	dai
reach the mark	-dai ni noseru
market	shijō
open-air market	aozora shijō
market order	nariyuki chūmon
marketable securities	yuka shoken
materials	genryō
	shiryō
	zairyō
raw materials	genryō
	genzairyō
medium term	chūkai

medium-term government bond funds	chūki kokusai (also chūkoku)
money market	tanki kin'yū shijō
municipal	chihō no
municipals	chihō jichitai saimu shōken

N

negotiated transaction	aitai baibai, aitai
new equity issue	shin-kabushiki
advance from new equity issue	shin-kabushiki haraikomi-kin
net	jun
fixed assets to net worth ratio	kotei hiritsu
total net worth	shihon gōkei
net profit	jun-rieki
net worth	jiko shihon
nominal par value	meimoku gakumen
	gakumen
non-consolidated	tandoku
non-fulfilment	furikō
non-observance	furikō
non-operating expense	eigyō-gai hiyō
non-operating profit	eigyō-gai rieki
note	tegata
notes payable	shiharai tegata
notes payable for facilities	setsubi kankei shiharai tegata
notes receivable	uketori tegata

O

obligations	saimu
failure to meet obligations	saimu furikō
obsolescence	chinpuka
ODR (official discount rate)	kōtei buai
offer	uri chūmon
offering	boshū
official discount rate (ODR)	kōtei buai
oil	sekiyu
crude oil	gen'yu
open order	mukigen chūmon
open-air market	aozora shijō
operate, operations	eigyō
	keiei
	sōgyō
operating costs	eigyō-hi
operating leverage	eigyō teko
degree of operating leverage	eigyō teko-ritsu
operating profit	eigyō rieki
operating volume	eigyō shūeki
operation	eigyō
	sōsa
stabilizing operation	antei sōsa
order	chūmon
buying order	kaitsuke chūmon
order without limit	nariyuki chūmon
ordinary	futsū

ordinary deposit	futsū yokin
ordinary discount	futsū waribiki
ordinary stock	futsū kabu
others	sono ta
overtrading	kaiten akinai
own	dokutoku
	jiko
	shoyū
own stock	jiko kabushiki

P

paper profit	chōbo-jō rieki
par value	gakumen
payable	shiharai
accounts payable	kaikake-kin
notes payable	shiharai tegata
pay-as-you-earn	gensen kazei
payment	bensai
	shiharai
per	-atari
per share earnings	hitokabu-atari no rieki
prepaid	maebarai
prepaid expense	maebarai hiyō
post office	yūbin-kyoku
post office savings	yūbin chokin
pre-tax	zeibiki-mae
pre-tax profit	keijō rieki

price	bukka
	daikin
	kakaku
	nedan
prefectural	chihō no
prefectural bonds	chihō jichitai saimu shōken
present	genzai
present value	genzai kakaku
principal	ganpon
principal repayment method	ganpon hensai hōshiki
procure	chōtatsu
production	seisan
reduced production	gensan
profit	rieki
	shūeki
appraisal profit	hyōka eki
book profit	chōbo-jō rieki
enterprise profit	jigyō rieki
	jigyō shūeki
gross profit	sō-rieki
	sō-shūeki
	uriage sō-rieki
marginal profit	genkai rieki
	genkai rijun
marginal profit ratio	genkai rieki-ritsu
net profit	jun-rieki
non-operating profit	eigyō-gai rieki
operating profit	eigyō rieki
paper profit	chōbo-jō rieki
recurring profit	keijō rieki
special profit	tokubetsu rieki
unrealized profit of instalment	kappu hanbai mi-jitsugen rieki
profit & loss statement	son'eki keisansho

135

profit before tax	zeibiki-mae jun-rieki
profit from asset sales	shisan shobun eki
profit from sales of property	yūkei kotei shisan shobun eki
profitability	shūekisei
	saisansei
profitability ratio	shūeki-ritsu
progress	hattatsu
	shinpo
construction in progress	kensetsu kari-kanjō
work in progress	shikakehin
property	bukken
	yūkei kotei shisan
profit from property sales	yūkei kotei shisan shobun eki
loss from property sales	yūkei kotei shisan shobun son
prospectus	mokuromi-sho
red herring prospectus	aka-nishin mokuromi-sho
purchase	baishu

Q

quick assets	tōza shisan
quick ratio	tōza hiritsu
quotation board	keiji ban

R

R&D	kenkyū kaihatsu
R&D expenditure	kenkyū kaihatsu hi
raise	chōtatsu
rally	hanpatsu
	modoshi
technical rally	aya-modoshi
range	fukin
ratio	buai
	hiritsu
	-ritsu
current ratio	ryūdō hiritsu
debt ratio	fusai hiritsu
fixed cost ratio	kotei-hi ritsu
liquidity ratio	ryūdōsei hiritsu
marginal profit ratio	genkai rieki-ritsu
profitability ratio	shūeki-ritsu
quick ratio	tōza hiritsu
turnover ratio	kaiten-ritsu
variable cost ratio	hendō-hi ritsu
raw	miseiren
	nama
raw materials	genryō
	genzairyō
real estate	fudōsan
rebound	hanpatsu
	modoshi

technical rebound	aya-modoshi
receive	**uketoru**
accounts receivable	urikake-kin
advance received	maeuke-kin
dividend received	uketori haitō-kin
interest received	uketori risoku
	uketori risoku waribiki-ryō
notes receivable	uketori tegata
recession	**fukeiki**
	fukyō
	fukyō-kan
recurring	**keijō**
recurring profit	**keijō rieki**
red	**aka-**
in the red	akaji
red herring prospectus	**aka-nishin mokuromi-sho**
reduced production	**gensan**
reduced profit	**gen'eki**
region	**fukin**
rent	**chinshaku ryō**
repayment	**bensai**
repurchase	**gensaki**
bond repurchase agreement	gensaki
bond repurchase market	gensaki shijō
research	**kenkyū**
research & development	**kenkyū kaihatsu**
research & development expenditure	**kenkyū kaihatsu hi**
research costs	**kaihatsu-hi shiken kenkyū-hi**
reserve	**jōyo**
	junbi
	tsumitate
capital reserve	shihon junbi-kin

retirement reserve	taishoku kyūyo hikiate-kin
reserve for debt	hikiate-kin
long-term reserve for debt	chōki hikiate-kin
reserve for bad debt	kashidaore hikiate-kin
reserved yen	tsumitate en
retained earnings	rieki-kin
unappropriated retained earnings	tōki mi-shobun rieki-kin
retirement	taishoku
retirement reserve	taishoku kyūkyo hikiate-kin
return	rieki
	shūeki
return on assets	shisan rieki
	shisan shūeki
revenue	shūnyū
accrued revenue	mi-shūnyū-kin
risk	risuku
risk arising from exchange rate fluctuations	kawase risuku

S

safety	anzen
sale	baikyaku
sales	hanbai
	shobun
	uriage-daka
cost of sales	hanbai hi
	uriage genka
loss from sales of asset	shisan shobun son

loss from sales of property	yūkei kotei shisan shobun son
profit from asset sales	shisan shobun eki
profit from property sales	yūkei kotei shisan shobun eki
samurai bond	endate gaisai
savings	chochiku
	chokin
post office savings	yūbin chokin
savings bank	chochiku ginkō
scarcity	shinausu-kan
securities	shōken
investment securities	tōshi yūka shōken
marketable securities	yūka shōken
security	anzen
	meigara
security capital	anzen shihon
security analysis	shōken bunseki
selling	hanbai
selling, general & admin. cost	hanbai-hi kanri-hi
selling order	uritsuke chūmon
settlement	bensai
	kessai
short allowance	tanki hikiate-kin
short-term	tanki
short-term borrowing	tanki kariire-kin
short-term loan	tanki kashitsuke-kin
sinking	gensai
sinking fund	gensai shikin
sinking funds bond	gensai shikin saiken
skyrocketing	ao-shijō
slow down	donka
slump	bōraku
small and medium enterprises	chūshō kigyō

Small and Medium Enterprises Agency	Chūshō Kigyō Chō
source	gen
	gensen
special	tokubetsu
	tokushu
special expense	tokubetsu hiyō
special loss	tokubetsu sonshitsu
special profit	tokubetsu rieki
speech	enzetsu
keynote speech	kichō enzetsu
spiralling	kyōran
spiralling price rises	bukka kyōran
spot	genbutsu
spread	bunsan
stabilising transaction, stabilising operation	antei sōsa
stability	antei
stable dividends	antei haitō
statement	keisansho
profit & loss statement	son'eki keisansho
stagnation	fushin
stock	chochiku
	kabushiki
	kokusai
subsidiaries stocks	kogaisha kabushiki
stock exchange	shōken torihikijo
stockholder	kabunushi
strong stockholder	antei kabunushi
stocks	zaiko
stores	chozō-hin
stop order	sashine chūmon
straddled order	sashine chūmon

141

straight bond	futsū shasai
strong	antei
	kyōryoku
strong stockholder	antei kabunushi
structure	kōchikubutsu
	kōzō
structural adjustment	kōzō chōsei
subsidiary	kogaisha
subsidiary stock	kogaisha kabushiki
support buying	ajitsuke, ajitsuke-gai
surplus	kuroji
sweetener	amami zairyō

T

takeover	baishū
	kyūshū gappei
tangible	yūkei
tangible fixed asset	yūkei kotei shisan
tariff	kanzei
tax	chōzei suru
	zei
	zeikin
	hōjin zei
accrued tax	hōjin-zei-tō jūtō-kin
before tax	zeibiki-mae
net pre-tax profit	zeibiki-mae jun-rieki
pre-tax profit	keijō rieki
technicality	aya

technical rally, technical rebound	aya-modoshi
technical reaction	aya-oshi
technical rebound	aya-modoshi
thin	usui
thin trading	akinai-usu
title	meigara
TNW (total net worth)	shihon gōkei
topless	ao-shijō
total	gōkei
	-kei
total asset	shisan gōkei
total liabilities & total net	fusai shihon gōkei
total net worth	shihon gōkei
trade	bōeki
trade deficit	bōeki akaji
rise in trade deficit	bōeki akaji kakuda
trade surplus	bōeki kuroji
trading	akinai
	baibai
	bōeki
trading for cash	genbutsu torihiki
trading volume	baibai-daka
transaction	baibai
	sōsa
	torihiki
date of transaction	baibai seiritsu-bi
negotiated transaction	atai baibai, (also) aitai
stabilizing transaction	antei sōsa
transfer	jōto
trillion	chō

turnover	baibai-daka
	dekidaka
	kaiten
turnover ratio	kaiten-ritsu

U

unappropriated	mi-shobun
unappropriated retained earnings	tōki mi-shobun rieki-kin
unconditional call loan	kōru mujōken mono
underlying bills	gen-tegata
underlying share	gen-kabushiki
underwriter	andāraitā
unfinished goods	han-seihin
unrealized	mi-jitsugen
unrealized profit of instalment	kappu hanbai mi-jitsugen rieki

V

variable	hendō
variable cost	hendō-hi
	kahen hiyō
variable cost ratio	hendō-hi ritsu

volume	-daka
	-ryō
operating volume	eigyō shūeki
sales volume	dekidaka
	uriage-daka
voting power	giketsu-ken
voting shareholder	giketsu-ken kabunushi

W

wasting	genmō
wasting assets	genmō shisan
work	kinmu
	seisaku
	shikake
work in progress	shikake-hin
working	unten
working capital	keiei shihon
	unten shihon
working capital ratio	ryūdō hiritsu
	unten shihon hiritsu
worth	kachi
	zaisan
net worth	jiko shihon
total net worth	shihon gōkei

Y

yen	en
reserved yen	tsumitate en
yield	budomari
	rimawari

PART • THREE

STATISTICAL
REFERENCES

NOTE

The tables appearing in this section are offered as general indicators of Japanese economic and financial activity and, as collated and analysed by the Japanese, they may be of particular interest to users of this dictionary; all tables are drawn from the international comparisons published by the Keizai Koho Center (Japanese Institute for Social and Economic Affairs), Tokyo, 1995.

LIST OF TABLES

TABLE 1
Value of Japan's foreign trade per capita and rate of dependency on foreign trade

	Value of Foreign Trade Per Capita (1993)[a]		Rate of Dependency on Foreign Trade (1993)	
	Exports (f.o.b., US$)	Imports (c.i.f., US$)	Exports	Imports
Japan	**2,913**	**1,943**	**9.2%**	**6.3%**
USA	1,823[b]	2,366	7.4	9.2
Canada	5,273	5,054	24.5	23.5
UK	3,115	3,493	18.1	21.0
Germany	4,494	4,058	24.0	22.8
France	3,641	3,510	18.0	18.0
Italy	2,961	2,596	15.6	16.5
Netherlands	9,219[c]	8,814[c]	43.8	42.0
Switzerland	8,505	8,220	24.4	24.6
Korea, Rep. of	1,884	1,919	26.0	27.8
Singapore	26,248	30,226	135.7	154.3
China, People's Republic of	77	88	18.5	17.5

a) Trade values have been divided by 1992 estimated population. b) f.a.s. basis c) 1992
Source: Bank of Japan, *Comparative International Statistics*, 1993

(US$ million)

TABLE 2
International trade matrix (1993)

Exports from \ Exports to	Japan	USA	Germany	UK	France	Italy	Industrialized Countries	Developing Countries	World Total
Japan	—	96,716	20,323	12,299	6,324	3,901	183,358	155,145	339,841
USA	47,764	—	21,236	22,808	14,581	8,698	261,827	181,426	447,400
Germany	9,363	27,371	—	33,328	55,768	39,942	341,501	77,640	429,290
UK	3,915	21,783	26,411	—	20,128	10,783	150,998	36,259	189,997
France	4,182	15,117	40,711	21,384	—	25,282	182,448	46,774	236,089
Italy	3,444	12,410	36,265	11,741	26,038	—	135,917	38,918	178,840
Industrialized Countries	97,827	315,671	295,102	172,149	200,537	132,820	1,961,300	653,778	2,656,300
Developing Countries	108,507	213,385	64,546	32,617	31,783	35,658	603,072	381,695	1,030,277
World Total	206,334	529,056	359,648	204,766	232,320	168,478	2,564,372	1,035,473	3,686,577

Based on f.o.b. customs clearance statistics
Source: Bank of Japan, *Comparative International Statistics*, 1994

TABLE 3
Retail trade in Japan by type of establishment (1991)

Type of Establishment	No. of Stores	Annual Sales (¥ billion)	No. of Employees (1,000)	Annual Sales per Employee (¥ million)
General Merchandise	4,347	19,898	440	45.3
Large-Scale Stores[a]	2,004	19,574	427	45.8
Dry Goods & Apparel	240,989	14,884	809	18.4
Food and Beverages	622,751	41,453	2,542	16.3
Motor Vehicles & Bicycles	93,230	18,934	566	33.4
Motor Vehicles	59,120	18,096	493	36.7
Furniture	158,104	11,977	587	20.4
Other	471,765	33,488	1,993	16.8
Drugs & Toiletries	90,845	3,963	272	14.6
Books & Stationery	76,730	4,722	600	7.9
Eating & Drinking[b]	510,101	9,720[c]	2,055	4.7
Sushi Shops	47,446	1,138	167	6.8
Coffee Shops	150,608	1,619	456	3.6
Retail Trade, Total	**2,101,287**	**150,354**	**8,992**	**16.7**

a) Including department and superstores that regularly have 50 or more employees
b) 1986   c) Excluding bars, cabarets, nightclubs, pubs, and beer halls
Source: MITI

TABLE 4
Balance of trade for selected countries

(US$ million)

	Japan	USA	Germany[b]	France	UK	Italy	Canada	Australia	Mexico	Korea Rep. of
1982	20.14	−36.44	24.73	−15.79	3.17	−8.91	14.99	−2.61	6.80	−2.59
1983	34.55	−67.08	21.42	−8.75	−2.38	−2.51	14.97	0.03	13.76	−1.76
1984	45.60	−112.52	22.14	−4.65	−7.11	−5.82	15.97	−0.88	12.94	−1.04
1985	61.60	−122.15	28.58	−5.28	−3.85	−6.08	12.57	−0.96	8.45	−0.02
1986	92.82	−145.06	55.75	−2.08	−14.06	4.53	7.68	−1.84	4.60	4.21
1987	96.42	−159.56	70.20	−8.67	−19.02	−0.34	8.96	0.26	8.43	7.66
1988	95.00	−126.96	79.77	−8.54	−38.16	−1.36	8.16	−0.71	1.67	11.45
1989	76.89	−115.68	77.75	−10.65	−40.54	−2.17	5.99	−3.44	−0.65	4.60
1990	63.58	−108.84	70.99	−13.67	−32.74	0.62	8.78	0.37	−4.43	−2.00
1991	103.09	−73.79	22.57	−10.18	−18.27	−0.90	5.16	3.53	−11.33	−6.98
1992	132.40	−96.14	32.32	1.70	−23.96	3.09	8.18	1.54	−20.68	−2.15
1993	105.80[a]	−132.47	43.13	8.40	−20.17	20.26[a]	9.86	−0.16	−14.02[a]	0.64[a]

a) Data: Up to 3rd quarter   b) Data on Germany covers both the former FRG and the former GDR as from 1990 III.
Source: IMF, *International Financial Statistics*, July 1994 and August 1993

152

TABLE 5
Exports and imports by commodity and country (1993)
(US$ million, customs-clearance basis, exports f.o.b., imports c.i.f.)

		Foodstuffs	Raw Materials	Fuels	Crude Oil	Chemical Products	Machinery Transportation Equipment	Motor Vehicles	Other Industrial Products	Total of Products
		(0,1)[a]	(2,4)	(3)	(333)	(5)	(7)	(78)	(6,8)	(5,6,7,8,9)
Japan	Exports	**1,884**	**2.300**	**1,601**	—	**19,061**	**243,147**	**78,410**	**66,304**	**328,511**
	Imports	**37,229**	**27,642**	**53,070**	**29,665**	**16,939**	**37,676**	**6,584**	**55,329**	**109,944**
USA	Exports	39,928	26,815	11,122	27	43,956	200,933	36,622	84,303	329,193
	Imports	30,372	16,393	58,662	41,200	28,886	237,068	77,052	162,921	428,875
Germany	Exports	22,077	8,935	5,285	22	54,278	213,535	71,540	119,721	387,534
	Imports	39,344	19,366	30,423	14,277	34,951	141,080	40,695	134,375	310,405
France	Exports	34,604	6,715	5,374	—	31,433	91,218	27,636	61,932	184,583
	Imports	24,206	9,020	20,561	9,728	26,348	83,313	23,157	74,715	184,375
UK	Exports	15,287	3,450	12,164	7,841	26,286	77,667	15,606	52,352	156,306
	Imports	23,646	8,966	12,306	6,599	20,461	83,334	21,341	70,539	174,334
Italy	Exports	8,863	2,455	655	14	12,508	61,382	13,120	77,175	151,065
	Imports	15,860	13,480	12,702	10,209	20,968	55,885	22,493	44,296	121,148

a) Commodity categories are based on SITC standards.
Source: OECD, *Foreign Trade by Commodity*

153

TABLE 6
Japan's merchandise trade by area (1981–1993)
(US$ million, customs clearance basis)

	Total Japanese Merchandise Trade			with USA			with EU[a]			with Middle East[b]		
	Exports	Imports	Balance	Exports	Imports	Balance	Exports	Imports	Balance	Exports	Imports	Balance
1981	152,030	143,290	8,740	38,609	25,297	13,312	18,894	8,552	10,342	17,732	42,670	-24,938
1982	138,831	131,931	6,900	36,330	24,179	12,151	17,064	7,560	9,504	16,946	37,764	-20,818
1983	146,927	126,393	20,534	42,829	24,647	18,182	18,523	8,120	10,403	17,160	33,796	-16,636
1984	170,114	136,503	33,611	59,937	26,862	33,075	19,405	9,334	10,071	14,206	33,066	-18,860
1985	175,638	129,539	46,099	65,278	25,793	39,485	20,016	8,893	11,123	12,171	29,937	-17,766
1986	209,151	126,408	82,743	80,456	29,054	51,402	30,675	13,989	16,686	9,795	18,427	-8,632
1987	229,221	149,515	79,706	83,580	31,490	52,090	37,693	17,670	20,023	9,177	20,197	-11,020
1988	264,917	187,354	77,563	89,634	42,037	47,597	46,873	24,071	22,802	9,438	19,602	-10,164
1989	275,175	210,847	64,328	93,188	48,246	44,942	47,908	28,146	19,762	8,559	23,054	-14,495
1990	286,948	234,799	52,149	90,322	52,369	37,953	53,518	35,028	18,490	9,877	31,336	-21,459
1991	314,525	236,737	77,788	91,538	53,317	38,221	59,158	31,792	27,366	12,312	29,331	-17,019
1992	339,649	233,021	106,628	95,793	52,230	43,563	62,474	31,280	31,194	15,206	29,246	-14,040
1993	360,911	240,670	120,241	105,404	55,236	50,168	56,412	30,149	26,263	13,256	27,234	-13,978

TABLE 6 (continued)

	With Southeast Asia			With Latin America			With Africa			With Communist Bloc etc.c)		
	Exports	Imports	Balance	Exports	Imports	Balance	Exports	Imports	Balance	Exports	Imports	Balance
1981	34,426	31,930	2,496	10,516	6,669	3,847	10,038	4,779	5,259	9,514	7,724	1,790
1982	31,873	29,985	1,888	9,086	6,268	2,818	6,930	3,740	3,190	8,401	7,430	-971
1983	34,548	27,988	6,560	6,391	6,462	-71	6,006	3,272	2,734	8,930	7,004	1,926
1984	36,795	31,883	4,912	8,549	7,230	1,319	4,838	2,776	2,062	10,602	7,982	2,620
1985	33,248	30,264	2,984	8,486	6,242	2,244	3,539	2,896	643	16,190	8,480	7,710
1986	41,788	29,489	12,299	9,494	6,194	3,300	3,533	3,585	-52	14,064	8,232	-5,832
1987	52,982	38,627	14,355	8,760	6,355	2,405	4,757	3,694	1,063	11,924	10,627	1,297
1988	67,109	47,802	19,307	9,297	8,313	984	4,806	3,944	862	13,818	13,863	-45
1989	73,516	52,906	20,610	9,381	8,871	510	4,609	4,078	531	12,643	15,584	-2,941
1990	82,721	54,601	28,120	10,280	9,851	429	4,886	3,720	1,166	9,842	16,977	-7,135
1991	96,176	58,810	37,366	12,793	9,838	2,955	5,211	3,692	1,519	11,943	19,115	-7,172
1992	104,373	57,516	46,857	15,841	8,720	7,121	5,035	1,725	3,310	14,577	21,207	-6,630
1993	117,425	60,592	56,833	16,915	8,359	8,556	4,439d)	1,817d)	2,622d)	20,444	25,376	-4,932

a) 1975–1980 Nine countries, 1981–1985 Ten countries, 1986 Twelve countries   b) Includes North Africa (Lybia, Egypt, Sudan, Ethiopia, Djibouti) and 16,952 in 1992 without S. Africa   c) Exports to China: 6,130 in 1990, 8,539 in 1991, 11,949 in 1992, and 17,273 in 1993 Imports from China: 12,054 in 1990, 14,216 in 1991, 16,952 in 1992 and 20,565 in 1993   d) Except South Africa and the North African countries
Source: Japan Tariff Association, *The Summary Report: Trade of Japan, December 1993*

155

TABLE 7
Japan's production and export of principal items (1993)

	Production (1,000) (A)	Exports (1,000) (B)	Ratio (B/A)
Watches [a]	389,392	37,426[d]	96.1%
Passenger cars	8,497	4,096[d]	48.2
Bicycles	6,867	110[d]	1.6
Video Cassette Recorders	15,846	16,415[d]	103.6
Colour TVs	10,758	5,667[d]	52.7
Microwave Ovens[b]	3,505	987	28.2
Washing Machines[b]	5,163	741	14.4
Electric Cleaners[b]	6,335	1,042	16.4
Electric Calculating Machines[c]	41,576	17,446[d]	40.7
Copying Machines	2,207	1,518[d]	68.8

a) Based on data of Japan Clock & Watch Association. b) Source: Electric Industry Association c) Table type only d) Source: Japan Tariff Association, *The Summary Report: Trade of Japan, December 1993*

TABLE 8
US merchandise trade by area (1981–1993)
(US$ million, adjusted on balance-of-payments basis, excluding military)

	Total US Merchandise Trade			with Japan			with EU[a]			with Latin America[b]	with Asian NIEs[c]	with OPEC nations
	Exports	Imports	Balance	Exports	Imports	Balance	Exports	Imports	Balance	Balance	Balance	Balance
1981	237,044	265,067	−28,023	21,788	37,590	−15,802	51,355	41,390	9,965	3,622	−6,098	−28,886
1982	211,157	247,642	−36,485	20,692	37,681	−16,989	46,904	42,340	4,564	−4,750	−7,338	−10,872
1983	201,799	268,901	−67,102	21,792	43,348	−21,556	47,746	45,767	1,979	−12,209	−12,353	−9,662
1984	219,926	332,418	−112,492	23,230	60,210	−36,980	49,944	57,784	−7,840	−14,338	−20,142	−13,078
1985	215,915	338,088	−122,173	22,148	65,653	−43,505	48,418	62,595	−14,177	−13,058	−21,028	−11,437
1986	223,344	368,425	−145,081	26,352	80,753	−54,401	51,841	74,163	−22,322	−10,184	−28,629	−8,507
1987	250,208	409,765	−159,557	27,630	84,578	−56,948	59,504	81,455	−21,951	−11,953	−34,786	−13,702
1988	320,230	447,189	−126,959	37,185	89,800	−52,615	74,464	86,036	−11,572	−8,583	−29,089	−9,239
1989	361,697	477,365	−115,668	43,864	93,531	−49,667	84,513	85,508	−995	−9,915	−26,274	−17,401
1990	388,705	497,558	−108,853	47,807	89,594	−41,787	96,284	91,353	4,931	−11,760	−20,472	−24,829
1991	415,962	489,398	−73,436	47,213	91,502	−44,289	101,278	85,700	15,578	−2,642	−14,833	−14,632
1992	448,165	532,664	−84,502	47,763	96,542	−48,779	102,845	94,050	8,795	414	−13,882	−11,026
1993	464,767	580,544	−115,777	47,950	107,268	−59,318	96,957	98,007	−1,050	−3,255	−12,008	−12,246

a) 1976–1980 Nine countries, 1981–1985 Ten countries, 1986– Twelve countries b) Brazil, Mexico anf Venezuela c) Hong Kong, Republic of Korea, Singapore and Taiwan

Source: US Department of Commerce, *Survey of Current Business*, March 1994

TABLE 9
Japan's leading trading partners (1991–1993)

(US$ million, except %)	Japan's Exports to –						Japan's Imports from –					
	1991	1992	1993	1991	1992	1993	1991	1992	1993	1991	1992	1993
USA	91,538	95,793	105,405	29.1%	28.8%	29.2%	53,317	52,230	55,236	22.5%	22.4%	23.0%
EU	59,158	62,474	56,412	18.8	18.4	15.6	31,792	31,280	30,149	13.4	13.4	12.5
Hong Kong	16,315	20,746	22,686	5.2	6.1	6.3	2,064	2,044	1,989	0.9	0.9	0.8
Taiwan	18,255	21,146	22,081	5.8	6.2	6.1	9,493	9,449	9,678	4.0	4.1	4.0
Korea, Rep of	20,068	17,770	19,115	6.4	5.2	5.3	12,339	11,577	11,678	5.2	5.0	4.9
Germany	20,605	20,309	18,021	6.6	6.0	5.0	10,739	10,738	9,786	4.5	4.6	4.1
China	8,593	11,949	17,273	2.7	3.5	4.8	14,216	16,952	20,565	6.0	7.3	8.5
Singapore	12,213	12,974	16,601	3.9	3.8	4.6	3,415	3,096	3,602	1.4	1.3	1.5
Thailand	9,431	10,366	12,261	3.0	3.0	3.4	5,252	5,947	6,502	2.2	2.5	2.7
UK	11,040	12,286	12,047	3.5	3.6	3.3	5,017	4,889	4,951	2.1	2.1	2.1
Malaysia	7,635	8,115	9,649	2.4	2.4	2.7	6,471	6,573	7,642	2.7	2.8	3.2
Australia	6,493	7,048	7,694	2.1	2.1	2.1	13,011	12,447	12,218	5.5	5.3	5.1
Netherlands	7,219	8,097	7,431	2.3	2.4	2.1	1,227	1,315	1,331	0.5	0.6	0.5
Canada	7,251	7,072	6,297	2.3	2.1	1.7	7,698	7,674	8,096	3.3	3.3	3.4

TABLE 9 (continued)

(US$ million, except %)	Japan's Exports to –						Japan's Imports from –					
	1991	1992	1993	1991	1992	1993	1991	1992	1993	1991	1992	1993
Indonesia	5,612	5,575	6,022	1.8%	1.6%	1.7%	12,770	12,244	12,478	5.4%	5.2%	5.2%
France	6,117	6,311	5,545	1.9	1.9	1.5	5,813	5,411	5,122	2.5	2.3	2.1
Philippines	2,659	3,516	4,814	0.8	1.0	1.3	2,351	2,333	2,380	1.0	1.0	1.0
Belgium	4,190	4,700	4,114	1.3	1.4	1.1	1,353	1,265	1,367	0.6	0.5	0.5
Saudi Arabia	3,893	4,841	4,087	1.2	1.4	1.1	10,081	10,190	8,887	4.3	4.4	3.7
Mexico	2,818	3,803	3,962	0.9	1.1	1.1	1,742	1,242	1,073	0.7	0.5	0.4
Italy	3,788	3,899	3,211	1.2	1.1	0.9	4,534	4,157	3,828	1.9	1.8	1.5
United Arab Emirates	2,154	2,728	2,534	0.7	0.8	0.7	10,524	9,742	8,948	4.4	4.2	3.7
Switzerland	3,008	2,800	2,144	1.0	0.8	0.6	3,629	3,184	2,828	1.5	1.4	1.2
South Africa	1,635	1,718	2,005	0.5	0.5	0.6	1,819	1,908	1,897	0.8	0.8	0.7
Brazil	1,226	1,139	1,624	0.4	0.3	0.4	3,180	2,846	2,848	1.3	1.2	1.1
India	1,523	1,486	1,529	0.5	0.4	0.4	2,190	2,037	2,277	0.9	0.9	0.9
Former USSR a)	2,114	1,076	1,501	0.7	0.3	0.4	3,317	2,402	2,769	1.4	1.0	1.1
Sweden	1,796	1,700	1,293	0.6	0.5	0.4	1,272	1,206	1,543	0.5	0.5	0.6
World, Total	314,525	339,649	360,911	100.0	100.0	100.0	236,737	233,021	240,670	100.0	100.0	100.0

a) Russian only in 1992 and 1993
Source: Japan Tariff Association, *The Summary Report: Trade of Japan*

159

TABLE 10

Share of major countries in world exports and imports (1981–1992)

(%)

	1981	1982	1983	1984	1985	1986	1987	1988	1989	1990	1991	1992
Exports												
Japan	**7.8**	**7.8**	**8.4**	**9.2**	**9.5**	**10.3**	**9.6**	**9.6**	**9.2**	**8.4**	**8.9**	**9.0**
USA	12.4	12.2	11.8	12.1	11.7	11.1	10.5	11.7	12.2	11.5	11.9	11.9
UK	5.3	5.5	5.3	5.1	5.4	5.2	5.4	5.3	5.1	5.4	5.2	5.0
Germany	9.1	9.9	9.7	9.3	9.9	11.8	12.2	11.7	11.4	12.0	11.4	11.2
France	5.5	5.4	5.4	5.3	5.4	6.1	6.1	6.1	6.0	6.3	6.1	6.3
Italy	4.0	4.2	4.2	4.0	4.1	4.7	4.8	4.6	4.7	5.0	4.8	4.7
Imports												
Japan	**7.3**	**7.2**	**7.2**	**7.2**	**6.9**	**6.2**	**6.2**	**6.8**	**7.0**	**6.9**	**6.7**	**6.2**
USA	14.0	14.0	15.3	18.4	18.6	18.4	17.5	16.6	16.4	15.1	14.3	14.7
UK	5.3	5.5	5.7	5.6	5.8	6.1	6.4	6.8	6.6	6.5	5.9	5.9
Germany	8.4	8.5	8.7	8.1	8.4	9.2	9.4	9.0	9.0	10.1	11.9	10.7
France	6.2	6.3	6.0	5.5	5.7	6.2	6.5	6.5	6.4	6.8	6.5	6.3
Italy	4.8	4.8	4.5	4.5	4.6	4.8	5.2	5.0	5.1	5.3	5.1	5.0

Source: Bank of Japan, *Comparative International Statistics*, 1994

TABLE 11

Japan's international balance of payments – IMF basis (1980–1993)

(US$ million)

	Current Balance	Current Balance (Trade Balance)			Services	Transfers	Long-term Capital	Short-Term Capital	Errors and Omissions	Overall Balance
		Exports	Imports	Balance						
1980	−10,746	126,736	124,611	2,125	−11,343	−1,528	2,324	3,141	−3,115	−8,396
1981	4,770	149,522	129,555	19,967	−13,573	−1,624	−9,672	2,265	493	−2,144
1982	6,850	137,663	119,584	18,079	−9,848	−1,381	−14,969	−1,579	4,727	−4,971
1983	20,799	145,468	114,014	31,454	−9,106	−1,549	−17,700	23	2,055	5,177
1984	35,003	168,290	124,033	44,257	−7,747	−1,507	−49,651	−4,295	3,743	−15,200
1985	49,169	174,015	118,029	55,986	−5,165	−1,652	−64,542	−936	3,991	−12,318
1986	85,845	205,591	112,764	92,827	−4,932	−2,050	−131,461	−1,609	2,458	−44,767
1987	87,015	224,605	128,219	96,386	−5,702	−3,669	−136,532	23,865	−3,893	−29,545
1988	79,631	259,765	164,753	95,012	−11,263	−4,118	−130,930	19,521	2,796	−28,982
1989	57,157	269,570	192,653	76,917	−15,526	−4,234	−89,246	45,830	−22,008	−33,286
1990	35,870	280,350	216,770	63,580	−22,190	−5,520	−53,080	31,540	−20,917	−6,587
1991	72,905	306,580	203,490	103,090	−17,690	−12,495	31,390	−103,240	−7,682	−6,627
1992	117,640	330,870	198,470	132,400	−10,140	−4,620	−30,780	−75,770	−10,458	632
1993	131,448	351,292	209,778	141,514	−3,949	−6,117	−78,336	−14,426	−260	38,426

Source: Bank of Japan: *Comparative Economic and Financial Statistics for Japan and Other Major Countries*, 1994

161

TABLE 12
Foreign currency exchange rates to the US dollar (1982–1994)
(national currency per US$, period average, except as indicated)

	Japan (Yen)	UK (Pound)	Germany (D. Mark)	France (Franc)	Italy (Lira)	Canada (Dollar)	Switzerland (Franc)	Australia (Dollar)	Korea Rep. of (Won)
1982	249.08	0.5713	2.4266	6.5721	1,325.5	1.2337	2.0303	0.9829	731.08
1983	237.51	0.6592	2.5533	7.6213	1,518.8	1.2324	2.0991	1.1082	775.75
1984	237.52	0.7483	2.8459	8.7319	1,757.0	1.2951	2.3497	1.1369	805.98
1985	238.54	0.7714	2.9440	8.9852	1,909.4	1.3655	2.4571	1.4269	870.02
1986	168.52	0.6817	2.1715	6.9261	1,490.8	1.3895	1.7989	1.4905	881.45
1987	144.64	0.6102	1.7974	6.0107	1,296.1	1.3260	1.4912	1.4267	822.57
1988	128.15	0.5614	1.7562	5.9569	1,301.6	1.2307	1.4633	1.2752	731.47
1989	137.96	0.6099	1.8800	6.3801	1,372.1	1.1840	1.6359	1.2618	671.46
1990	144.79	0.5603	1.6157	5.4453	1,198.1	1.1668	1.3892	1.2799	707.76
1991	134.71	0.5652	1.6595	5.6421	1,240.6	1.1457	1.4340	1.2835	733.35
1992	126.65	0.5664	1.5617	5.2938	1,232.4	1.2087	1.4062	1.3600	780.65
1993	111.20	0.6658	1.6533	5.6632	1,573.7	1.2901	1.4776	1.4704	802.67
1994[a]	107.62	0.6723	1.7242	5.8620	1,684.8	1.3413	1.4533	1.4128	808.25

a) Average of 1st quarter
Source: IMF, *International Financial Statistics*, July 1994